I0464315

The 7 Laws of Real Estate

A Guide for New Investors

William Tappan

The 7 Laws of Real Estate
A Guide for New Investors

William Tappan

ISBN 13: 978-1481947480
ISBN 10: 1481947486

Edited by Molly and Jim Cameron of Cameron Editorial Services, mj.edit@cox.net

Thanks to Alli Von Mohr for bringing the cover together.

Books by William Tappan
Real Estate Exchange and Acquisition Techniques (1978)
The Real Estate Acquisition Handbook (1979)
Real Estate Exchange & Acquisition Techniques (1989)
Handbook for the Financial Analysis of Real Estate Investments (1993)
Available at Amazon.com
Real Estate Acquisition: 150 Techniques for Serious Investors (2012)
The 7 Laws of Real Estate: A Guide for New Investors (2013)

For

Zachary and Paul

Contents

Chapter 1

The First Law

Buy a Place to Live

Develop a sense of place. All of us have a place where we belong. It is a strong pull and easier for some to feel than others. It is where you want to buy a home, live, and enjoy the daily gifts that make a happy life. Some realize it with time and familiarity. Others are lucky by birth and are connected from the start. Some never find this sense or realize the meaning of where they are.

A few years ago, I was talking with a friend who had emigrated from South America. She had lived in different states during her time in this country: married, raised a family, became a citizen, and built a productive and accomplished life. She told me that, as she drove into New Mexico for the first time, a certainty came to her: it was a quiet comfort that this is where she belongs and she knew it as soon as she crossed the border with Texas.

Knowing with this degree of clarity is rare. Most of us are not that aware, but perhaps we can be. Stop and ask if you are taking your place for granted. Do you realize what defines and makes your surroundings unique? Do you understand the history and appreciate the past that shapes the place where you live? Can you build on the experiences of those who were there before you? Can you improve and add value to the area and make a contribution to those who follow?

—

Setting up a Headquarters

You probably thought I was going to tell you to buy a house to live in. You're right, I am. But it's more: start with a sense of place that informs your choice and helps you make decisions you can be proud of. Then find a base to work from for real estate acquisition. Initially, it might be a rental house or apartment, but it should provide security as you ride into the unknowns of real estate investment. To work efficiently within the place you choose, you need what we in the West call a headquarters.

Decades ago, during the summers between college semesters, Ben and I would drive to Idaho and work in the Clearwater National Forest. We had a base camp of tents outside a small town that depended on logging for employment. The days were spent in the forest in an attempt to control white pine blister rust. In the evening, we split wood for the stoves that provided heat for the tents in this damp forest.

After supper we would go into town. There were three churches and five bars in this little logging town of 525 people. The largest bar and cafe was called the Headquarters. Over the mirror on the bar wall there was a sign: "I Would Rather Be Healthy and Rich than Sick and Poor."

Sometimes simple words capture deep meaning. Developing a sense of place, setting up a headquarters, and having your primary objectives in perspective are the cornerstones of a good foundation to build a real estate acquisition program.

The headquarters is where you can learn, plan, and rest—a place where you can be out of the battle before the next foray into the wilderness of the market.

—

Keeping in mind why you are venturing into real estate is always important: enough money for independence from an employer and cash flow that you control are both worth considering. They are a good start toward financial security and stable income. Fortunately, real estate is an effective vehicle for reaching these objectives while providing the foundation for much more. Specify what you want. Think about your goals and the reasons for doing this.

Financial security dominates any thinking person's investment objectives, regardless of net worth. It is the elephant in the living room of our debt-ridden society. For some, it goes beyond reason to a greed for more with no understanding of why.

An individual who is tranquil in the knowledge of what is enough is rare and fortunate. With a little perspective, the peace that comes from realizing when you have enough can put you ahead of most people, and give you a risk-aware basis for making investment decisions.

Satisfaction in life comes from what you accomplish, not from what you acquire. These might seem strange words in a book on real estate — but maybe less so when you understand that real estate is only a vehicle to take you to your destination. Develop at least a general picture of where you want to go with real estate. Investing is a means to a larger goal, not an end in itself. The following is your map. How you use it is your choice.

Facing Anxiety

It takes effort for some people to overcome the anxiety of buying real estate. Embarking on a first commitment can be nerve racking. But it is really a lack of familiarity that goes away with exposure, as is the case with many new challenges. Anxiety is the first barrier. Some barely notice it and move on. Others drag it around like an anchor. If you are troubled by the prospect of ownership, take a little time and ask yourself, "What is the worst that can happen?"

Defining the downside is a good way to escape anxiety. My brother told me a story of a first-home-buyer couple he guided through the process. Initially, they were paralyzed with fear to the point of being unable to make a decision. Their anxiety translated into an inability to determine which house they even liked. Blinded by the overwhelming prospect of grasping the details of all the choices, they froze. The wife cried. The husband walked in circles.

After a few months, they made a decision and bought their first home. The chemicals of anxiety gradually left their bodies and they went forward, becoming familiar with the new world of home buying. Ten years later, the wife who cried over making a decision was a successful real estate agent, and the husband who walked in circles was a successful home builder.

All it took was a little time and familiarity to overcome a formerly daunting challenge. They found courage — the ability to take action in spite of fear.

The really good thing for this couple was that their learning, and the ability to overcome anxiety, resulted in careers in real estate. Many people have overcome anxiety before you, and many will do it after you. You can do it too.

Other barriers often are money for a down payment and an understanding of the financing process. One of the characteristics of real estate is its credit dependence.

An all-cash purchase, although common in some circles, is not part of the expected home purchasing process. There are many government programs designed for first-time buyers. Temporary buying incentives are frequently injected into the market, depending on the condition of our political economy. Private financing is common in many areas of the country. A good real estate broker can help navigate the financing requirements.

And that is how you buy a house: find an experienced broker, listen carefully, and remember what you hear. No one gets through this process without help. When you first start, ask for help. It's yours for the asking.

Simplifying the Documents

All professions have specialized terms that describe their activities. Learning what these words mean is the first step toward familiarity. Understanding follows when you know the effect of the described activities on you — the rights and obligations that define your responsibilities, and underpin your future action.

Paperwork can be boring, but we live in a FIRE-dominated economy (Finance, Insurance, Real Estate), and much of it involves pushing through paper to get to real function and utility.

Equally important, knowing the meaning of some of the basic terms can help reduce the anxiety of a first purchase. Here are the basic documents you will encounter:

Purchase Agreement. A meeting of the minds of buyer and seller is negotiated in writing. No agreement in real estate has legal standing unless it is in writing. This is where the structure of the purchase takes shape. In its most basic form, the purchase agreement transmits offers and counter offers between the parties. It brings the conflicting desires of price and terms to clarity on paper, where the final agreement is signed and ready for processing. Buyer and seller sign the purchase agreement.

Title Insurance. The title company that closes the transaction generates a title insurance policy, insuring the condition of the title, and listing any exceptions to the coverage. As part of the process, the buyer is furnished a title policy binder prior to closing for review and approval. The title binder lists problems with the title that may be exceptions to the policy. It will also state whether a current survey is required for title insurance purposes. The binder is issued before closing. The policy is issued after closing.

. Title companies often require a current survey to make sure there are no encroachments on the property. For example, did a neighbor build a wall that comes onto the property? A survey is useful because it is a picture of the dimensions of the property. It helps make sure that what you are getting is the same as what you expect to get. Walking the property before closing, with survey in hand, to check the location of the corner stakes is always a good idea. Review and approve the survey before closing.

Settlement Statement. The settlement statement lists the documents involved in the transaction and accounts for the money involved: the loans, down payment, proration of property taxes, loan interest, and municipal services (water, sewer, and garbage) and miscellaneous fees. This is the document you can use to learn basic real estate accounting and understand how the numbers balance to complete a closed transaction. Buyer and seller sign the settlement statement.

Loan Documents. Usually, the lender or bank prepares the loan documents. These disclose the details of the loan, including the interest rate and the term (length of time) of the loan. They consist of a note and mortgage or, in some states, a deed of trust; both perform the same function. The note is the promise of the buyer to pay the loan amount. The mortgage secures the loan and is recorded as a lien against the property. Buyer signs the note.

Warranty Deed. The warranty deed conveys the rights and obligations of ownership from the seller to the buyer. It contains the legal description of the property, which may refer to a platted subdivision or consist of a metes and bounds description delineated by a surveyor. The seller signs the deed.

Miscellaneous. Several other documents are typical in a transaction, depending on the purchase agreement terms and state law, and location of the property: buyer disclosure of the property condition, home inspection report, and septic inspection, if the property is in a rural area without sewer service.

Other documents are needed as the complexity increases, but this list covers the basics. Understand these and you will make a good start. As you move from buying houses into buying apartments, commercial property, and land investments, the requirements and paper work will increase, as will your real estate vocabulary and your understanding of the process.

Understanding Ownership

When you complete a purchase, you have an equity position. The lender who financed the purchase has a debt position. Your job now is to protect your equity by keeping the mortgage payment up to date and maintaining the condition of your property.

Real property is a fee interest, which includes a bundle of rights: the land surface, attached buildings, mineral rights, water rights, easement rights, leasehold rights, option rights, air rights (above the land), and more. For our purposes, it is enough to know that there is a lot more to real estate than meets the eye. That's what makes it ever more interesting the deeper you get involved.

There are two popular methods of investing in real estate. One is direct: you can acquire an equity position, which is what most people think of. The other is indirect: you can acquire a financial instrument secured by real estate. There is about one degree of separation between owning real property and a financial instrument secured by real property. Both are capital assets. Both generate cash flow.

Furthermore, financial instruments secured by real estate are virtually as common as equity ownership because most properties are purchased with loans. Loans are investment interests in real estate for lenders because loans are secured by real property, even though they are financial instruments (notes and mortgages) rather than actual real estate. When you buy property—an equity investment—your silent partner is the lender who has a debt investment. In that sense, you never completely own property until you pay the loan in full because the lender has a claim against the property.

One of my first commercial sales was land owned by someone who used to live in town. He was heir to the real estate business his family built, and had long ago moved to the beaches of California. His late mother was connected politically. Her specialty was buying property for back taxes and she managed to acquire a large portfolio of land and rentals. Usually, she would hold property for a few years and sell it on a real estate contract, which is similar to a note and mortgage. When I met her son, the portfolio consisted mostly of real estate contracts, which provided substantial cash flow.

The son retired early, but returned to town to sell a city block, which was part of several properties he still owned. I was able to sell it and, in the process, bought a couple of rentals from him with nothing down. All he wanted was cash flow — he wasn't concerned about cash up front.

As we drove around town, he would point out property, saying "I own that, I own that." When I asked if he would sell one of them to me, his reply was usually, "No, it's still paying." I bet the people paying thought they owned the property. But in his mind, it was his, even though all he had was a real estate contract.

A real estate contract (financial instrument) conveys equitable title while formal title (the deed) is held in escrow, pending full payment of the debt. When the loan is paid, the warranty deed is released to the buyer by the escrow agent and recorded. The buyer then becomes the formal owner by deed, although for all practical purposes he already was the owner.

This type of financial instrument is administered differently than a note and mortgage, where title is conveyed at purchase and repossession is relatively complex. The real estate contract is unique in its ease of foreclosure, which makes it popular for privately financed sales. On default, the seller is given a special warranty deed by the escrow agent, which conveys all rights of ownership back to her. Many states have similar instruments called by different names such as land sale contract.

Mortgages and real estate contracts are two financial instruments that work on the debt side of real estate. Knowing the debt instruments of real estate is important for an appreciation of the risks inherent in ownership. The foreclosures working through our society reflect a lack of risk awareness and understanding by many at all levels of the process.

Looking for Property

Now you know the importance of a headquarters, understand the basic terminology, and recognize that real estate consists of many interests and rights. The next step is usually acquisition of residential rental property.

It could be that you buy a rental house or one with an attached apartment or a duplex. All the choices lead to cash flow, which comes in many forms and can move in two directions. But to capture cash flow, you must first find property to buy.

Pick an area you feel comfortable with and drive around the neighborhoods from time to time and look for property that is for sale. Make a call and start negotiations. Look at ads online and in the newspaper.

If you come across a group of apartments that are not advertised but attract you, go to the county assessor's office or your title company, find the owner, and call. Establish a working relationship with a broker and you will probably have more choices than you can handle.

First, make sure you acquire property that provides cash flow to you, or at least breaks even from rent and has potential. Avoid property that takes cash flow from you. Try to find property that makes sense at first glance and is likely to benefit from growth.

Look in older areas that are coming back in popularity and are in the process of being gentrified. If you are good with your hands, fixer-up property in a reasonable location can be profitable. The key is to find property that fits your energy level and management capacity.

In my hometown, there is an area with a lot of rentals called "the war zone" by local brokers. Ownership turnover is high, and there is always an inventory of property with worn-out owners ready to sell. There is another area known as the edge of the war zone. This is where new investors and people from out of town often start their investment adventure. Many of these are people lacking patience. More accurately, they are people who don't want to take the time and make the effort to find better property—they just want to buy something. There is a better approach.

Acquiring real estate requires work and persistence. Consider your choices carefully. Try to find property compatible with your capacity to handle the demands ownership will place on your time and money. There is such competition for choice property that it is helpful to approach the process with a central question in mind: Will this acquisition improve my position? Be flexible and keep a broad view of the market. There is often opportunity where you least expect it.

With that thought in mind, it is useful to divide the opportunities you find into three groups: Group A for long-term investment; Group B for short holdings for trade when Group A properties show up; Group C for trading in anticipation of finding a buyer who specializes in that type of property.

With each type of property, the price and terms determine the risks and benefits. Each group warrants a different financial structure. You can pay a little more for Group A. Group B requires a built-in price advantage to ensure a profit when you trade. Group C must be acquired with care and at the most advantageous price.

Establish your intention when you acquire property. Clarity at that time will help when you eventually sell or exchange.

Negotiating the Acquisition

Much of success in life comes from learning to trust your instincts, even when you are new to an investment activity. It is a strange experience to know a certain property is part of your future even before you own it. Learning to listen to your intuition and taking action on it is a real skill. It can lead you into some good transactions and it can keep you out of trouble.

When you find property you want, start negotiating. Learn to make negotiation your default state of mind. Always be negotiating. Make it part of your body language. Be calm, poker faced, polite, curious, and questioning. Make "Let me think about it" your stock answer — and then do it.

Cultivate this demeanor from day one with everyone you meet, including your own real estate agent. No one needs to know what you are thinking, or if you want a certain property. They all will find out soon enough when you sign a purchase agreement. You are in a very important game of poker here and it is always best to keep the cards close to your chest.

You might find that good terms come to you if you are quiet — and I mean almost nonresponsive. If someone wants to sell you property and you want it, just let the seller or the agents talk until the terms adjust in your favor. Be around. Be interested. Be curious. But develop an attitude that ranges from "I don't have to buy this" to "I might let you convince me to buy it." Concurrently, work out what makes financial sense regarding price, income, vacancies, and expenses, and try to guide any discussions toward terms that make sense for you.

Listen to what the seller wants. Determine the underlying interests that resulted in the property being offered for sale: Is the owner tired of management? Does the owner want to leave town? Are there personal or financial reasons for the sale?

When you have a good picture of the owner's underlying reasons for selling, you may be able to structure a purchase to meet those interests while also meeting your own: Are you planning to pay a nominal down payment? Would a higher interest rate offset the low down payment? An acquisition that provides high interest on a seller-financed transaction has real value.

When we think of negotiation, a picture of an offer and counter offer, give-and-take process comes to mind — but it is so much more. If you can keep in mind that real estate is a vehicle for improving your financial position, you can easily see that the same is true for the seller.

Search for improvement is the underlying motivation of the parties in most transactions. Discover those interests in yourself and the seller and you have a chance of alignment and a successful negotiation. It is not necessarily about money.

For example, an owner who takes pride in her property wants to know that the new owner will also. Price under this scenario may be secondary to completion of the seller's vision. Land development that completes the plan for a long-held property can mean more to the seller than the money received from the sale.

If you are unable to reach an alignment of interests with the seller, don't give up. With time the situation could change. For that reason, always keep your options open and never dismiss the relationship you have established. It may just be the start of a better opportunity than you thought possible. Although you may move on to another acquisition, keep a link to the one that got away. It might come back to you in a way that makes even more sense.

Reviewing Operations

Verifying income, vacancy, and expense history is a must before you close. Ask for a reasonable amount of time to check and approve the books. It is up to you to make sure the reality of the property is as close as possible to your expectations.

This involves getting into the detail of daily operations, as reflected in the numbers associated with the property: Has the rent been paid regularly? Has the rent been raised over the years? Have there been periods of extended vacancy? Are the expenses steady and consistent? What is the condition of the property? Will you need to make capital improvements, and when? Try to be as thorough during your inspection as you would be for a house you planned to live in.

Going through this process doesn't have to be a big deal. It is just a first step in becoming familiar with the property and how it operates as a cash flow producer. Sometimes the best indicator is what you find wrong. Little errors in management and maintenance can be inexpensive to correct but have a highly profitable impact.

What expenses will increase after you buy? Will property taxes increase because of your purchase? Will property insurance go up? Look at its history and to the future. Try to uncover the unexpected.

Much of the rental property for sale suffers from deferred maintenance. Neglected maintenance or overdue capital improvements may be signs of an owner bleeding the property for short-term gain at the expense of long-term value. The net operating income may seem high, but make sure it is not the result of deferred maintenance.

Worn out owners make bad managers. This will show up in the vacancy rate and the way the property is managed. Maybe the rent is too high for the value offered. Maybe consistent attention to maintenance would warrant an increase in rents and result in the property operating at potential. Sometimes the best buys are properties operating below potential that can be improved with strong management.

Vacancies are such a waste. They are losses that can't be recovered. When you rent to a tenant, you sell time. Time can't be recovered.

Income lost to vacancy because the asking rent is above the market rent can never be recaptured. It is very important to minimize vacancies by being competitive, maintaining your property, and paying attention to daily management. Ask yourself if the property you buy at the price you pay will allow you to operate competitively.

*****

Understanding Compound Growth

The most basic understanding of the time value of money starts with awareness of the risk of cash flow lost to time. It shows in rent missed for one month or two or more and it shows in lost property value when the market turns against you before you can sell.

I have seen owners who are sure they have a bankable million and borrow in anticipation of a sale, only to see their property repossessed by the bank because they priced the sale just a little above the market and wouldn't budge when prices started falling. It is very important to develop awareness of how the market works and how fast it can change.

The time value of money has real meaning when vacancies hit or when you miss a chance to sell just before the market turns down. These basic risks of investing are best understood in terms of time and the interruption of growth.

Compound growth is central to the operation of your property. When you have a vacancy, you not only lose a month's rent, you also lose the interest on the reinvestment of that rent. It is not added to your capital base so it can go to work earning money. This loss of earning power is in addition to the loss of cash flow and the property value it supports.

Past growth is lost to time when the value of property drops. It may come back, but that recovery from a lower level is growth only to your starting point, requiring precious time just to get back to where you were. When you are back to that point, profitable growth can start again.

For example, if the price of your property drops by 50 percent, you may consider it a 50 percent loss. But to recover that loss, the property must appreciate 100 percent from the new value just to reach the old value. It must double. This is a somewhat extreme example, but not farfetched, given the price fluctuations in some areas. It illustrates a primary investment principle and a reason to time and price your acquisitions carefully. Always try to control your losses by investing and managing your property with an awareness of real estate cycles.

It may be impossible to predict the time needed to recoup a loss, but you can calculate with ease how long it will take to double the value of an investment at certain rates of growth. An amount that grows at 10 percent compounded monthly will double in 7 years. In the above example, the property value will take 7 years to double and get back to the original starting amount if it grows at 10 percent.

This useful rule of 70 is the result of the following formula. Divide the number representing the percentage rate of growth into 70 and you will have the years required to double: (70 / 7 = 10) or (70 / 10 = 7). This rule of thumb is specific to monthly compounding. You can accomplish the same result for annual compounding by dividing the numerical value of the growth rate or interest rate into 72. This is referred to as the rule of 72.

So now you can see how long it will take to double your savings at the interest rate on a certificate of deposit. For example, a 1 percent CD will double in 70 years: (70 / 1 = 70 years). Not so good for savers.

Financial security and a stable income from investments are inseparable from a reasonable growth rate. This is the positive side of compound growth, regardless of the rate of growth.

The negative side is debt at a high interest rate that just keeps increasing the amount you owe. Understand

———

23

that debt doubles under the same compounding rules by which equity investments grow. Both sides of this equation require careful attention. A credit card balance with a 22 percent interest rate will double in just over 3 years if the payments are not made: (70 / 22 = 3.18 years). Not so good for borrowers.

Much of the growth in real estate takes place out of sight. You don't get a monthly statement for appreciation. Any clue to the growth of your real estate can come only from your understanding of the operations within the context of the changes in local market conditions.

Investing in Land

Land endures. Buildings wear out. Land may shift and change, but as long as there is the planet Earth there will be land. Land investment can be one of the most effective ways to store value and transfer purchasing power through time.

Land appeals to wealthy investors for several reasons: scenic beauty, potential for farming, grazing cattle, and a time-proven track record of holding value.

Over the years, large land holdings have formed the core of wealth protection for old money. There is no reason it can't do the same for you.

An acre near town that is inexpensive but in the path of growth is a good place to start. If you have extra income that you want to save, consider a small land purchase. Think of it as 1000 shares of stock in a good company that you are buying on time. Frame it as a savings account that you make deposits in each month.

Look for individuals who are selling land in likely growth areas. Work out a purchase that doesn't require much cash and has a low interest rate on a private land sale contract or real estate contract. Be patient and pay it off. Then look for another parcel.

Property taxes should always be calculated when considering land investment. Often, taxes are low when the investment is remote and years away from residential or commercial development. That's what you want to find in order to keep the carrying costs as low as possible.

Fortunately, agricultural and grazing exemptions serve to lower taxes when the property is put to productive farm use. Farm land has gained investment appeal through funds designed for wealthy investors who want to preserve purchasing power and the related protection from inflation. This investment effort has resulted in the purchase of timber land and large tracts of prime farm land for investment. In some cases, the land produces current income from farm production and lumber harvesting.

Remember that land tends to hold its value, requires little or no maintenance, and is a good hedge against inflation. And with planning, you can keep the carrying costs low.

Following the First Law

1. Put down roots and avoid jumping from residence to residence.

2. Put effort into investment activity, not shopping activity.

3. Understand that the return you get is a dollar amount.

4. Understand that the rate of return is an annual percentage.

5. Fear and anxiety are no match for understanding and knowledge.

6. Negotiation is a process of aligning the interests of the parties.

7. Compound growth is the foundation of all investing.

Chapter 2

The Second Law

Learn to Measure Cash Flow

When you think of cash flow and real estate, rental income is likely to come to mind. But cash flow from real estate has several sources; rental income is only one of them. For example, if in the future you refinance your home and take out money, you have realized a cash flow. It didn't come from income property, nor did it come from rent, but it is still cash flow from real estate.

Real estate has an advantage over most types of investments because of its flexibility and the opportunity for control and personal initiative. Equally important is the financial structure of real estate. When you refinance, the cash proceeds come from the loan balance you have paid down, and possibly from value appreciation. Equity buildup and appreciation are two benefits that produce cash flow when you refinance or sell.

Simplifying the Benefits of Real Estate

Cash flow is the result of the benefits of real estate. It is the measurable outcome of ownership and it flows in two directions. When things are going well, it is cash flowing from the property to you. When things are not going well, cash flowing from you to the property is more likely.

If you have to pay money to keep the daily

---

operations working smoothly, you own a negative cash-flow property that doesn't cover monthly expenses and debt service. But this is not necessarily a bad investment if future cash flow is likely from the other benefits of appreciation, tax shelter, and equity buildup.

Each real estate investment should be compared to the alternatives available in the financial markets. Which is safer? Which is more likely to improve your financial security? Maybe a negative cash flow property such as land is best viewed as a savings bond that you plan to sell and withdraw appreciated value from in 10 years.

For example, land can appreciate, compounding each year. It is not taxed until you sell. Dividends paid on stocks and interest paid on bonds are taxed each year when held in a conventional brokerage account.

Which will produce the higher risk-adjusted return: land in your market area bought for cash, or a bond with rock-bottom interest rates bought for cash? Understand that the price of a bond declines as interest rates rise, which is typical during inflation cycles. There are many ways to look at any investment. Sometimes the way you frame the view can produce a new perspective, allowing you to see value or risks you may have missed before.

Rental income is the first benefit of income property. It produces net operating income after vacancies and expenses. And when you subtract debt service, you are left with net cash flow that is money in your pocket, or a loss, which is negative cash flow out of your pocket.

Appreciation is the second benefit of real estate. It produces cash flow when you sell or refinance. If property values fall during your ownership, this benefit becomes stagnant. It can take years for appreciation to catch up to the purchase price and produce a profit if the cycle turns against you.

———

Tax shelter is the third benefit of real estate. It produces cash flow each year by sheltering a portion of your ordinary income from tax. For example, if you have an operating loss of $5,000 and an effective tax rate of 20 percent, that represents an annual cash flow of $1,000 ($0.20 \times \$5,000 = \$1,000$). In other words, you pocket $1,000 that would have been paid in tax. Multiply the loss by the effective tax rate to get the cash flow produced by the deduction.

Equity buildup is the fourth benefit of real estate. Each month, as the loan principal is reduced, your equity in the property grows. It is realized as a cash flow when you sell or refinance. The benefit is clear when viewed as a savings account with deposits made from rent—each property you own represents a separate savings account with deposits made monthly by tenants. There are few investments that you can borrow money to buy and know that someone else will pay off the debt.

RATE is the way to remember these four benefits of real estate: Rental income, Appreciation, Tax shelter, and Equity buildup. These are the sources of cash flow.

Moving from Benefits to Cash Flow

Rental income is easy to measure. Spreadsheets are useful tools when you want to develop an understanding of a property's financial performance over time. Here is a simple way to start by using annual performance:

Scheduled rental income: $14,400
Less vacancy (10%): $1,440
Effective rental income: $12,960
Less operating expenses: $3,000

Net operating income: $9,960
Less debt service: $8,246
Cash flow from rent: $1,714

At this point, you have the information you need to establish the capitalization rate (cap rate) on this property. The cap rate is determined by dividing the net operating income (NOI) by the price. This formula allows you to compare the performance of various rental properties on a similar basis.

For example: $9,960 divided by $160,000 equals a cap rate of 0.0623, or 6.23 percent. This is an annual percentage that represents the rate of return from rent over one year, before debt service, compared to price. It is the rate of return you would receive if you paid cash for the property.

Armed with this information, you can easily see how the property you are considering compares with other properties by comparing each based on the percentage return before debt service. Just look at the cap rate. It shows how property is priced based on income, which helps you make a decision prior to considering the specific terms for the financing the property.

When you know the prevailing cap rate in your market, you can divide it into the NOI of any property to see if the offering price is high or low in comparison to other property on the market ($9,960 divided by 0.0623 equals $159,872, rounded to $160,000).

It is also possible to measure appreciation — the price increase that supports the real estate market when the cycle is going in a positive direction. It is the result of demand in a growing local economy. You can calculate it by monitoring the sales prices of similar property.

Purchase price: $160,000
Loan: $128,000
Equity: $32,000

Annual estimated appreciation: 3.5%
Appreciation at end of one year: $5,600 (0.035 x $160,000 = $5,600)
Appreciated value: $165,600
Appreciation return on equity: 17.5% ($5,600 / $32,000 = 17.5%)

Note that appreciation is calculated based on the total value of the property, but the percentage return is calculated based on the cash invested or down payment. This is leverage at work. You invest $32,000, and it grows based on the increase in total value of the property, which starts at $160,000. So it is really the percentage growth of the total property value that compounds. That growth is then added to the cash invested or down payment in the form of compounded equity. This is how leverage works — you use debt to magnify the increase in appreciated equity.

Tax shelter can be measured as well. It is the result of depreciation of the improvements, not the land, associated with rental property. This is the area where a good accountant is invaluable, but it is important to understand the processes involved.

Cost basis: $160,000
Less land value: $16,000
Equals improvements value: $144,000

Improvements depreciated over 27.5 years equal a

deduction of $5,236 per year.

See *IRS Publication 527* if you are interested in learning more detail than you might find enjoyable. This soft deduction is an expense item each year, which offsets rental income. The cash flow comes when this deduction combines with other deductions to produce a loss on your annual tax return. Note that this calculation starts with net operating income (NOI) and deducts the interest and depreciation for the first year. The principal portion of the debt service is not deductible.

Net operating income: $9,960
Less interest: $6,357
Less depreciation: $5,236
Equals taxable income (loss): ($1,633)

These calculations represent first-year performance. During subsequent years, the interest paid will decrease because it is calculated on a lower loan principal. Keep in mind that it is also possible to have a negative NOI when effective rental income is low and expenses are higher. Now we can determine the cash flow represented by this first-year loss:

Taxable loss times effective tax rate equals cash flow of $327:
(0.20 x $1,663 = $327)

Determine the cash value of any deduction by multiplying it by your effective tax rate, not by your marginal bracket. Calculate the effective tax rate by dividing the tax you paid for the year by gross income.

Equity buildup from loan reduction is the principal

———

payment portion of debt service paid during the year. In this example, that amount is $1,888.

Summary:

Rental income: $1,714 (actual cash flow after expenses and debt service)

Appreciation: $5,600 (unrealized potential based on a 3.5 percent annual estimate)

Tax shelter: $327 (actual cash saved from taxes by deductible loss)

Equity buildup: $1,888 (principal portion of debt service resulting in loan reduction)

Measure the first-year performance in this example by ignoring the unrealized potential of appreciation and focusing only on the actual cash results of the first year. This amount is $3,929, represented by the rental income, tax shelter, and equity buildup. When divided by the $32,000 equity (down payment), this first-year performance represents a 12.28 percent cash return before appreciation. ($3929 / $32,000 = 12.28%)

Each year, the numbers will change, but you can use the same method to monitor the progress of your property. Keep in mind that the actual cash flows from the benefits are spread out over time:

Rental cash flow is ongoing.

Appreciation is realized on refinance, sale, or exchange.

Tax shelter is ongoing.

Equity buildup is ongoing but realized on refinance, sale, or exchange.

Owning rental real estate comes with a built-in

———

tendency to balance risk. When one benefit is not performing as you might like, one of the others may take up the slack and offset the damage.

Risk adjustment is inherent to the benefits of real estate and important to your future investment return and financial security. Calculating cash flow before buying is just using common sense.

Understanding Appreciation

Real estate does not always appreciate. Neighborhoods and entire cities can and do fall into decline. If you could buy without analyzing your choices and simply sit back to enjoy the appreciation and income that are sure to follow, there would be fewer laws of real estate.

In our illustration above, the largest contributing benefit is appreciation. It is also the most elusive and the one most dependent on future events. Monitoring annual appreciation is an exercise in observation. Rental income, tax shelter, and equity buildup all represent actual dollar amounts that can be specified for a given year.

Appreciation is always an estimate and at best a statement of probable gain until it is realized on refinancing, sale, or exchange. Until then, you can use projections only in an attempt to follow this all-important benefit. Since it is likely to be such a large contribution to your financial security, it warrants attention.

Patience is your best choice when you invest in real estate. If you are fortunate to buy at the right price, and in a good location within a community that has growing employment, monitoring appreciation can be a comfort.

———

With that positive thought, let's apply the rule of 70 to see what is necessary to double the value in this example.

If you find after a year or so that the appreciation in your investment area is 4.5 percent, how long will it take for your rental to double? Answer: 15.56 years (70 / 4.5 = 15.56 years).

If you think that is a little too optimistic, given the economy and market today, try a more conservative appreciation rate of 3 percent. This is the amount commonly attributed to long-term inflation. Answer: 23.33 years (70 / 3 = 23.33 years). This means that if you hold on for a little more than 23 years, you will have an asset worth $320,000 that you bought for $160,000, if it appreciates at 3 percent. This represents monthly compounding. Try the calculation using the rule of 72 to see how long it will take to double with annual compounding.

We apply appreciation rates to the value of property to measure the increase in price. But that is not the most important element; the down payment, which is the cash investment you make, is what grows or compounds and is the basis for determining the rate of return.

For example, the $32,000 cash investment grew to $160,000 by virtue of property appreciation—a 500 percent increase because of leverage (borrowed money). Without leverage—a cash purchase—the increase would be only 100 percent: $160,000 invested producing $160,000 in appreciation.

Appreciation is not some steady force that works on value every year. It is sudden and it is gradual; it is significant and it is minor, depending on the supply-demand interaction of the market and the stage of the real estate cycle.

Working with Leverage

Finding ways to increase leverage is a major part of real estate investing. Nothing down with no personal liability on a property that is not performing for reasons you can easily correct is as close to an ideal acquisition as any investor can find.

Under these conditions, measuring a rate of return is secondary to counting your bounty of good luck; and risk is left behind to be defined by the excessive debt and high price paid by some other buyer.

Last year, my friend Sonny sold a rental house to a couple with nothing down on a nonrecourse real estate contract. This was the happiest couple you could imagine. They had been through some hard times, but were employed and very appreciative of the opportunity to own a house. The tight credit requirements resulting from the housing and credit collapse had prevented them from buying through conventional channels.

For my friend, this couple was the perfect buyer, because they were fully committed to caring for the house and capable of making the payments and demonstrated an appreciation for the opportunity that engendered trust. That's all he needed.

Monthly income for retirement with a higher interest rate than possible in the financial markets was his objective. In fact, he required a clause in the contract that prevents early payment. Sonny didn't want cash. He wanted interest on his capital. So in exchange for nothing down, he got a high interest rate that will likely provide income for the rest of his life.

This story illustrates what is possible. It is a myth that a large down payment is the only way to offset risk.

You can find property without being forced to pay a large down payment. Often the financing is private and requires no bank approval. How do you find this type of high-leverage high-return property? You make a commitment to do the work and you start looking. Maybe it will take getting to know a few sellers or their brokers. There are many techniques for acquiring real estate and all-cash purchase is only one of them.

In most areas of the country, there have always been shadow banking systems operating in private financing, making loans and buying and selling mortgages. They are the market's answer to restrictive credit conditions imposed over previous decades.

Private financing wasn't as necessary during the easy credit conditions in the seven years prior to the 2007 housing cycle peak. But lately the pendulum is swinging back, and the use of private financing is growing in markets where loan underwriting standards have become tight again.

In a way, this is a good thing. It opens the door to alternatives for structuring acquisitions that can increase leverage without new bank financing. Often private financing will involve the seller carrying a second mortgage or real estate contract and the buyer assuming the first mortgage. Sometimes a wraparound mortgage or real estate contract is used. Depending on the terms of the existing first mortgage, this may or may not require bank approval.

As credit conditions tighten, alternative private financing methods are likely to become more popular and widely used. This means greater flexibility in negotiating with owners, possibly higher leverage, and terms tailored to individual circumstances.

Understanding the Cash Flow of Deductions

Some deductions are useful. Some cost more than they are worth. Depreciation of property is intended to allow replacement of capital assets using money not diminished by tax.

Government allows deduction of depreciation based on a theory of doing what is in the greater good: productive assets keep our economy going and should be replaced without loss of value due to tax on that portion worn by use and time. This way, the capital base of the economy is renewed, resulting in jobs and a growing economy.

Deduction of home loan interest is based on a similar theory. Home ownership results in a more stable country and is encouraged by government in many ways. But having a loan with deductible interest is not an end in itself and should not be valued as more than the initial incentive it is. Keep in mind that the government can take away any deduction at any time.

Depreciation on the improvements of rental property is a forward-looking deduction that has no direct out-of-pocket cost; but, deduction of loan interest has a cash cost. The question is: How much is the cost and how much is the cash flow? To answer this question, let's look at the cash flow of rental property depreciation and compare it with a home loan interest deduction.

Property depreciation of $5,236 has a cash flow benefit of $1,047 if you pay a 20 percent effective tax rate. (.20 x $5,236 = $1047) For the sake of example, let's say you just happen to pay $5,236 in interest on your home loan, which would produce the same cash flow amount when you take the deduction. What is the cost of each deduction?

Property depreciation costs you zero dollars. The interest rate deduction costs you $5,236, or a net-out-of pocket cash flow of $4,189 ($5,236 - $1,047 = $4,189). You paid nothing for the depreciation-related cash flow, but you paid $5,236 for the home interest deduction.

That's a big difference and a reason to pay off your home loan sooner rather than later. Paying interest is as much a waste as vacancies when the interest is paid on a loan that is not earning a return by facilitating an investment.

Note that your effective tax rate is calculated by dividing the tax you paid for the year by your gross income (all of it) before any deductions or credits. For example:

Total gross income: $100,000
Tax actually paid: $20,000
Effective tax rate: 20% ($20,000 / $100,000 = 20%)

Home loan interest paid for the year: $10,000
Times effective tax rate: 20%
Equals cash value of interest deduction: $2,000

In this example, you pay $10,000 cash to get $2,000 in cash.

A loan on your house may have some benefit if it places you in a lower marginal tax bracket. It certainly makes sense if it allows you to avoid paying rent. But otherwise, it costs more in interest than you are getting from the deduction and you should devise a plan to accelerate an escape.

For example, each year, you can pay down the

principal on your loan by as much extra as you feel comfortable doing. And the next time someone says something is tax deductible, you can calculate how much it will cost to buy that treasured deduction.

It's not how much you make, it's how much you keep that makes you financially secure. Capturing cash flow over time is the road to financial security. Pay off your home and gain the cash flow paid to the mortgage.

When you pay off any debt, your cash flow increases by the amount of the former loan payment. That new cash flow coming to you can then be invested as you choose.

Buying a rental house every year or so and paying off the loans on each of them before you retire can make you a millionaire, if that's what you want. Appreciation on a well-placed parcel of land can do the same thing. There are many ways to build an estate. Paying interest on nonproductive loans is not one of them.

The key is to get started and keep at it consistently. All of this takes time, perseverance, and the patience to live through the ups and downs of our chronically unstable political economy.

Using Interest or Being used by Interest

Paying interest makes sense when you earn more on the borrowed money than you pay in interest on the loan, provided the risk is manageable. This is smart leverage.

But carrying a high interest balance on a credit card used to buy nonproductive assets certainly makes no sense. That's just playing into the hands of our financially-engineered society that seems to intentionally guide people into never-ending debt. Big finance today is engineered to capture cash flow from interest and fees. Stretching out loan payments has become more important than payback of the loans. Financing of cars, student loans, and credit cards are all good examples to avoid. Interest-free loans can be the exception.

If anything, you want to be on the other side of the trade. For example, if you were to buy an apartment complex with no money down on a privately held interest-only real estate contract due in 7 years, you may be able to accomplish the following: the rental income could pay operating expenses and interest on the acquisition debt; the interest and expenses are deductible and could cancel the tax on the rent; any excess depreciation would produce a loss and indirect cash flow by sheltering other income; profit would come from a sale before the 7-year due date or by exchanging or refinancing based on the appreciated value.

This is the basic leverage model used to gain control of real estate, or a business, by using the operational profits in a tax deductible way to facilitate capital gain over time. It works because interest is deductible. It works because the operational rents or business profits are just enough to cover expenses and interest. And it leads to capital growth through appreciation without an initial investment. It is an old real estate structure that is also applied by private equity firms to acquire businesses for resale with interest-only financial instruments. It works for many savvy financial operators and it can work for you.

It makes sense to pay interest to acquire investments that generate cash flow. Paying interest on your house might be wasted money, depending on the interest rate and the rate of appreciation.

If you have a very low interest rate and a high

---

appreciation rate, you might be able to break even or make a profit. You're probably thinking that this is in conflict with the idea of paying off your home loan, because surely your home will appreciate. It probably will if you bought at the right time and for the right price. But will it appreciate fast enough to offset the interest cost?

Look at it this way: You buy a house for $230,000 with $30,000 down and a loan of $200,000 for 30 years at 6 percent. The interest cost over that 30-year period is $231,676. Let's say, for example, you sell the house after 30 years for $460,000.

    Purchase price: $230,000
    Plus interest paid: $231,676
    Equals total Cost: $461,676
    Less sales price: $460,000
    Equals difference: ($1,676)
    Plus tax savings on interest: $46,335
    Equals net profit: $44,659

The cash flow of the interest deduction based on tax savings is $46,335 with an effective tax rate of 20 percent (0.20 x $231,676 = $46,335). This can be viewed as reducing your interest cost to $185,341 ($231,676 - $46,335 = $185,341). In other words, you paid $231,676 in interest and got back $46,335 in tax savings. That's an incentive to pay off the loan faster.

Or you could view it as a forced savings account that produced $460,000 at the end of 30 years. There are many ways to frame this example. The best is the one that makes sense for your individual situation. Remember, 80 percent of the interest paid in this example goes to the benefit of the lender.

The interest rate in this example may seem high or low, depending on the stage of the credit cycle we are in. It's just an illustration of how interest costs can get away from you when there is no offsetting investment cash flow.

Now, we have two models for interest payments. The first is the financial model engineered to lever deductible interest into capital gain. The second is the consumption model used to acquire a needed good with the danger of paying twice for it when the interest charges are considered. One makes financial sense. The other doesn't, but may have the personal benefit of renting capital so you can eventually own a home.

Interest is a form of cash flow. It is the cost of money, and it can work for or against you. Ultimately, it is rent on capital. The challenge is to rent money that makes money, or alternatively to stop paying interest (rent) quickly and own the capital asset rent free. Keep an eye on interest and you'll learn the difference between investment and consumption.

Avoid adjustable-rate mortgages (ARMs). They contain nothing but surprises in an economy with chronically low interest rates. With fixed-rate mortgages you can project your debt-service requirements. With ARMs you never know what might happen or what is in the fine print. Their resets in the mid 2000s were a major factor in the failure of home loans taken out by a trusting public, lured into the trap by teaser rates.

Owning real estate is an opportunity to get on the right side of the cash flow-extraction society that is growing in our country. You want to collect rent, not pay it. You want to collect interest, not pay it. They are both rents. In the real estate world, rent is paid to the owner of property and interest is paid to the owner of the financial instrument secured by property. At times in your investment life, you may be both an owner of property and collector of rent, and an owner of financial instruments and collector of interest. Strive to collect rent and interest and avoid paying either.

However, when you first start investing, paying rent for a while may be your only option. And paying interest for investment purposes makes sense when the return on the invested capital is more than the interest paid for the capital. That is leverage.

Understanding the Cash Flow of Land

There are 43,560 square feet in an acre. There are 640 acres in a section and a section is a square mile, 5,280 feet on each side. Lots are often measured in square feet. Ranches are measured in acres. Big ranches are measured in sections.

Once, a fellow from back east bought some land in the southeast part of the state. He was buying some supplies in the local mercantile store and getting to know his neighbors. The store proprietor introduced him to a rancher who was also buying supplies.

The newcomer said to the rancher with a tone of pride, "I just bought a 180-acre ranch north of town. How many acres is your ranch?" The rancher said, "I don't know. I never figured it out." The proprietor started grinning as he noticed the puzzled look on the face of the new man in town. The rancher asked for a paper and pencil and said, "Let's see, it's 53 1/2 sections times 640, so that makes 34,240 acres, more or less."

It's all a matter of scale when it comes to figuring land values. Many years ago, a wealthy investor bought 500 acres. This acreage was miles from town, but in the path of growth. He paid four cents a square foot and sold it 5 years later for 15 cents a square foot. Ten years after he sold, the land was subdivided and offered at a dollar a square foot without zoning, city approvals, or infrastructure. By that time, the original investor had moved to California and when I met him on a return trip he refused to go anywhere near the land he used to own. The memory of selling too soon was above his pain threshold. In his mind, he had left a fortune on the table.

For example, his purchase price was $1,742.40 per acre times 500 acres, for a total of $871,200. He sold it for $6,534 per acre times 500 for a total of $3,267,000. However, had he held on (he didn't need the money), he could have eventually sold it for a dollar a square foot, or $21,780,000 ($43,560 x 500ac = $21,780,000). He never recovered from his seller's remorse.

The financial beauty of land is that, usually, the smaller the subdivided unit, the higher the square foot price. Cash flow comes from land sales and land leases. There was a successful oil man who had gas stations around town. He invested in land, which was well located for commercial use. When approached by a commercial user to sell, he always insisted on a land lease instead. Over the years, he built up quite an inventory of land and quite a cash flow from land rent.

For example, if the land was valued at $4.50 a square foot, he would negotiate a lease based on 10 percent of the land value per year. A 20,000-square foot lot valued at $90,000 brought in rent of $9,000 per year, or $750 per month. The lease always included rent escalation clauses based on increases in inflation or increases in the appraised value of the land.

There is a centuries-old practice of renting land to tenants for farming with rent paid by a share of the crop.

Today, as cities have overtaken farmland, the practice of leasing land for production of profits has survived. Only the tenants are different. Leasing land is a method of securing cash flow without selling. It is a long-term holding method that also produces current cash flow.

Following the Second Law

1. RATE will help you focus on the four benefits of real estate.

2. Benefits are measured by cash flows.

3. Cash flow comes in many forms—estimate it before purchase.

4. Appreciation is likely to be the source of the largest single cash flow.

5. Leverage is central to real estate investment, but must be used carefully.

6. Don't be fooled by deductions. Do the math.

7. Rent and interest are for receiving, not for paying.

Chapter 3

The Third Law

Watch the Fundamentals

We were having lunch with a young couple a few weeks ago. I had just given these friends a copy of my book on acquisition techniques. We were talking about prices and I said that $85,000 sounded like a very good price and I knew of a house that sold in California for that amount. It was purchased from a bank and word is the neighborhood is upset because it brought down the comparable sales data for the other houses. My friend countered that he had found some townhouses for sale in a gated community in Las Vegas for $40,000 about a year ago. He knows the area and was thinking about looking to see if any were still available.

Here we have an indication of the glut of housing in areas hardest hit by the credit expansion, overbuilding boom, and collapse in 2008. It is also a lesson in the importance of buying at the right price for the phase of the cycle currently in force. In many cities there is an overhang of repossessed housing and commercial property that will take years to clear. This consequence of easy credit, predatory lending, and fraud has distorted the market and will continue to until the excess inventory is cleared from the books of the lenders.

Wall Street speculators have started moving into the hardest-hit areas, as banks have sought to unload the end result of their bad loans. Vulture funds are buying foreclosed subdivisions filled with lots ready to build on and groups of houses they intend to rent for a few years and then sell.

What does work for a fast profit is buying wholesale from banks and selling to retail customers at the new lower market price. Banks make this possible by writing down their foreclosed property loans so bulk buyers can resell at current prices. Sales happen when new condos are priced at 60 percent—or less—of the original sales price. It seems hard to go wrong when the price is well below the cost of replacement. That's how price creates demand. In real estate, liquidity is a function of price—the lower the price, the more liquid the property.

Understanding the Economics of Real Estate

Demand for real estate can only be understood relative to supply. Together they make the market. It just doesn't make sense to consider one apart from the other. What might seem to be an overbuilding of apartments may be too few when compared to growing demand. The market is not static. Supply and demand fluctuate constantly as they flow through time cycles, attempting to achieve balance in face of over speculation, over borrowing and panic.

Demand comes from population growth and new household formations, combined with immigration from other states and countries. People are attracted to areas where there are jobs. Employment opportunity and an increasing population support healthy growth—without jobs, the population and the demand for real estate both shrink. Retirement and resort communities are exceptions.

Household income determines the quality and size

of the houses in an area. Interest rates support demand, stimulating it at low levels and stopping it at high levels, relative to household income. Credit availability and prevailing interest rates directly affect demand. Historically low interest rates from 2000 to 2007 and loans, made without regard to household income, were major factors in the housing bubble that preceded the crash in 2008.

Supply naturally increases in response to demand, as developers try to capture the profits promised by population growth and new household formations. Speculators first enter as excitement builds and again when prices fall, attempting to capture profits on the way up and after they hit bottom.

Price is the referee between supply and demand. High prices both attract supply and limit demand. The absorption rate is the crucial measure of market strength. This is true with new apartments, building lots, single-family houses, offices, and retail centers.

Can developers buy and finance land, get the necessary approvals, and develop buildable lots with roads, water, and sewer, then sell to builders and investors before the interest and carrying costs on the land outrun absorption of the product? Answering this question is a prerequisite to successful real estate development. It is also fundamental to understanding the economics of real estate. The key is the absorption rate, which is demand for supply in relation to time.

A large tract of land sold at the top of the market cycle in the mid-2000s. At the time, I just didn't see how the market could absorb the inventory fast enough to pay the interest on the debt used to acquire the land. And that was prior to the interest on the loans to develop the infrastructure necessary before the land could be sold as developed lots. Don't even bring up the delays that are routine during the approval process, including the request for state-sponsored bonds for infrastructure development. On its face, the economics just didn't make sense for this market at the top of the residential cycle.

When a very successful development company spends $180 million to buy 55,000 acres, financing most of the acquisition with debt from a big global bank, you would think they knew what they were doing. Maybe it will be a good venture for the company that bought it out of foreclosure for $148 million two years after the original sale. But that first purchase couldn't support the carrying costs. The new owner may have less debt in the deal and the market could turn around. We'll see if the economics work better during the next cycle.

This seems an extreme example in a book for new investors, but it is here for good reason: No matter how much money you have made, you are never immune to the economics and the cycles of the market. Also, no matter how much money and experience you have, you are still human and subject to mistakes.

None of us is immune to bad luck. The key is to avoid getting in a position that will prevent you from recovering from a mistake. And when it comes to our political economy, try to structure your life so that, no matter what happens, it will not interrupt your chosen lifestyle.

There is really no substitute for staying in touch with the local market. This means following the direction of new development, which is the leading edge of growth for any city. It also means learning about the areas that are deteriorating and the location of commercial areas with long-empty buildings that were once on the leading edge, perhaps decades ago.

And even more important, it means learning the neighborhoods that have completed their decline and are on the upswing in popularity with young buyers. These areas of opportunity being revitalized by new household formations contain desirable property at prices that may allow for upside potential.

Determining the Life Cycle of an Area

There is a life cycle to an area of a city. And within areas, there is a life cycle to neighborhoods. Areas usually are loosely defined and labeled by the subdivision name of their original plat, or by where they are or what they are near—a stadium, country club, river, intersection, hill, ravine, railroad, valley, north, south, or university.

Over time, an area forms a personality and takes on characteristics that create impressions in the minds of the residents throughout the city. These impressions are based on the age of the area, the condition of the houses and commercial centers, the demographics of the residents, and the position of the area in the life cycle of its real estate.

As new families form, demand for housing grows, construction responds, and the borders of a city expand. Sewer, water, and roads blaze the trail, followed by the traditional pioneers—churches. When you see a lone church on a newly built road, it can be a clue that subdivisions and commercial development will follow. A new road and a new church mark the edge of growth. That is a clue for land speculation in anticipation of the houses and commercial centers to follow.

None of this happens without underlying job growth. Jobs mean people and new families. The opposite is also true: cities that have lost major employers and are unable to replace them are in danger of becoming impoverished semi-ghost towns. Stable cities are dependent on an employed population. Growing cities are the result of a growing job base and the expanding population that follows.

As a city expands outwardly, it declines inwardly. Newness is a basic value in our country, and the desirable houses and shopping centers are those that are new or renewed. However, older established neighborhoods can trump distant new subdivisions. And this is an opportunity for investing in locations that are convenient and close. These are areas where older buildings retain and gain value because of their location. Shorter driving time to work and shopping or school and university has appeal.

The aging cycle within a city includes demolition or removal of older buildings to take full advantage of the location. In all cases, the decision to buy, buy and remodel, or buy and demolish, rests on the stream of future cash flows indicated by each option.

Timing is the major factor in new areas and old. Is new construction too far ahead of demand? Has the decline stopped in the older area and the gentrification process started, or is it likely to start soon?

The life cycle of an area within a city can be seen in the age and condition of the buildings and the attitude of residents. Figure out the impression of the public regarding an area, and then watch for changes over the years. Look for young couples moving to older areas — the renewal process that starts with new families.

*****

———

Understanding Real Estate Demographics

Demographics track the movement of people through time, placing them in groups by specifying their characteristics, usually with the intent of selling a product or service. It determines the employment and age of a population and much more. For purposes of real estate, as you can tell by now, employment and income level are core factors. It's not just employment, but the income level provided by the employment that defines the nature of an area's real estate market.

Once I met with a group that had developed software to determine the likely success of a commercial development in a specific location in the city.

It had population density, income characteristics, traffic flow, schools, and existing developments, and more, all defined in one easy-to-use program. It all made you wonder how anyone made a decision without the software. Certainly this is valuable information, but being on the ground in the middle of the market as it unfolds can be just as effective, if not more so.

Population age, employment characteristics and the trend of both is sufficient demographic definition to give you insight into the nature of an area within your city. The key is to be aware of the influence of these factors on your cash flow.

For example, if you acquire a couple of duplexes in a university area, it stands to reason that your tenants will likely be students. When classes end for the year, you need to consider, prepare for, and prevent the vacancies that might occur during the summer between semesters. In this case, your rental demographic is composed mainly of students and your cash flow may, in part, be tied to the school year.

Suppose you exchange one of your duplexes for a 12-unit apartment complex outside the entrance to a military base. Your rental demographic is now primarily military personnel and civilian workers on the base. It seems like a good trade because when you raised the rent by $10 on your duplex, total cash flow increased by $20 per month. With the 12 units, a $10 increase will provide a monthly increase of $120.

However, new concerns come with the new location and demographic. There are articles appearing in the paper about possible base closings or cutbacks that could affect your cash flow.

Maybe you can offset some of the risk by trying to attract tenants who are not dependent on the base for employment. Diversification into a different city with a totally different demographic might balance the risk.

You see that some apartments in a mining town about an hour out of town — if you drive fast — are available. Mining of this particular mineral has been slow for a little more than a decade, and rentals are in trouble and priced to sell. Rumors are just starting that some of the mines are being prepared for expanded operation. So at the right price and terms, you become the single largest owner of apartments in town. The mines are up and running within a couple of years, your apartments are full, and new ones are being built.

Now your rental demographic consists of employees dependent on a single industry. But your overall portfolio is diversified between minerals and military, and university with your plan being that all won't contract at the same time.

This example, taken from an actual investor experience, illustrates the role of demographics and how highly defined it can be. Each location depends on a different source for jobs and tenants. The tenant age here was relatively young, ranging from 18 to 30, as is often the case with apartments, but defined by the nature of the work and school.

A better way to diversify involves avoiding extreme dependence on any one employer by focusing on middle-income apartments that appeal to single tenants and families of all age groups. The location brings its own demographic characteristics. And the location that appeals to multiple demographic groups is likely to be the most stable investment — often near good schools and shopping.

Price and availability drive acquisition. It is important to invest where you feel comfortable and can deal with the nature of your tenants. But when you are starting on your real estate acquisition career, it is often the availability and price of a property that matter most, rather than the employment, income level, or age of the tenants. Nevertheless, demographics are central to real estate and are becoming an increasingly important factor as the population ages and the general income level of the country continues to decrease.

Using Price and Vacancy to Track Fundamentals

When supply increases beyond the ability of demand to absorb it, prices eventually adjust so the excess inventory can clear from the market. Banks are often involved in this process as foreclosures mount during the down cycle. With lower prices, buyers enter and activity picks up, demonstrating once again that liquidity in real estate exists when the price is low enough to attract demand.

Since prices express the fundamental balance of

supply and demand, it stands to reason that if you follow price changes, you can you track changes in the fundamentals. This works with houses and the rental rates of apartments: House prices go up when demand exceeds supply, creating a demand market. House prices go down when supply exceeds demand, creating a supply market.

When apartment vacancies are high (an oversupply of apartments), you may see incentives like a month's free rent or lower move-in costs (deposits and prepaid rent). Low vacancies mean owners not only end the incentives, but also become choosy about tenants. More stringent credit requirements become the way to screen tenants, all of whom may, in practice, be equally reliable. But higher credit standards and income level requirements are methods of allocating the scarce supply.

Comparing Houses and Apartments

Extreme turmoil in the housing market can produce extremes in the apartment market. Both market segments share many of the same participants. Traditionally, apartments have tended to serve as way stations on the path to home ownership. Now, they also serve as the stopping point after leaving home ownership due to foreclosure, as former homeowners wait for a new chance.

The foreclosure aftermath of the credit fraud and collapse of 2008 revealed a pattern of interaction between foreclosure and apartment rental activity. As single-family housing defaults increased, apartment demand surged. People who couldn't afford to make mortgage payments on too-big and too-expensive houses left them for apartments.

The ultimate result was an increase in multifamily construction in an attempt to meet the new demand. This is not demand from new households; it is demand from disrupted households, which combined with normal apartment demand from families unable to qualify for home loans under the new restrictive loan requirements.

Employment stability is the requirement for the shift from apartments back to home ownership. Recovery of the job market is a prerequisite to the housing recovery. Exit from the collapsing, over-built and over-borrowed housing market to apartment life is relatively fast in the slow-moving real estate market. The move from apartments back to homes is not as sudden.

Homebuyers who can't qualify for loans add to the demand for apartments. Rents increase until they hit the price at which buying a home is a better alternative. There is a competition between rentals and home ownership that is governed by credit availability and interest rates for purchase of a home.

This relationship shows in rental rates compared to the monthly payments of comparable homes. As rental rates increase to the point that buying makes more sense, tenants strive to become qualified buyers to avoid high rent.

Extremely low interest rates help to lower the monthly payments on home loans. However, it takes time to build up savings when banks suddenly require 20 percent down payments. Over time, bank requirements and high down payments become distant memories as the credit cycle swings once again toward easy loans.

*****

———

Using Brokers to Track Fundamentals

The single best way to stay in contact with the changing fundamentals of the real estate market is to establish relationships with competent real estate brokers. Their livelihood depends on knowing the market in depth and they are the first to sense change as it is happening.

An increase in the time houses or commercial buildings are on the market before selling, or a drop in phone calls on advertised properties, are front-line indicators of reduced buying and selling activity. Market activity contains the sum total of the fundamental forces of the real estate market.

When activity dries up, you know demand is dropping and it's a good bet that supply will continue to accumulate as builders complete projects already under construction. A drop in traffic through model homes is the first sign that absorption is about to change. Real estate brokers working independently, and for builders, know this is happening as it is happening.

They have real-time local statistics and a daily experience with the components of those statistics before a slowdown or increase in activity are common knowledge. Your fastest learning channel is a friend in the business you trust. Establish a relationship with a broker who you sense has your best interests in mind.

This will allow you to track market activity in real time and help in your investment planning and timing. Keep an eye on changes in market activity.

Reviewing the National Fundamentals

We live in a world of debt. It almost seems that we have outrun our ability to earn the revenue necessary to

---

pay the principal on our collective debt. In many areas of the nation, we have built and bought more houses than we can pay for at our current employment levels.

Fortunately, some cities have recovered and are experiencing reasonable growth trends. Others seem stuck, as if the major employment driver was the construction boom itself (Las Vegas, NV). When construction ended, employment ended, and it just can't seem to increase enough to absorb the excess housing inventory.

National housing prices are in a continuing down trend, and at times seem to be bouncing along the bottom. Maybe a bottom is at hand—and maybe not. Each city has its own numbers; together, they can paint a bleak picture if you choose to see it that way.

A better approach is to realize that the real estate market has a long history of ups and downs, and this down cycle is one of many. It is, however, more extreme because it is the result of regulatory negligence, widespread fraud, and financial manipulation. The result was a world-wide credit collapse rather than the periodic inventory contraction that has been more common. Being extreme, it will require more time to recover. And that gives you more time to find a good buy.

The excess supply of housing created during the first half of the 2000s had more help than normal from the credit industry. Real estate, including housing, depends on access to financing. It is an equity market that depends on debt to survive. Consequently, when credit is easy, prices tend to increase.

Real estate demand is also constrained by debt other than real estate debt. For example, total consumer debt restricts a borrower's ability to qualify and his capacity

---

to make payments on a home loan. Consumer debt and student loan debt, now weighing heavily on our society, prevents new household formation, which affects demand for homes.

Always, there is a point at which high prices choke off demand. Always, there is a point at which big debts can't be paid. When those points in price and debt are reached at the same time, the market collapses of its own weight. It can happen in stocks and bonds, gold and silver, and all forms of real estate. It just happened to be real estate's turn in the mid-2000s to learn basic market dynamics—what goes up can actually come down on a national level.

Down is where you buy for bottom dollar. It is not a time to give up hope and shrink from the market. Step back when prices increase beyond fundamental value due to easy credit. That is when you want to sell at top dollar and wait for reality to overcome human folly. Wait until the banks choke on foreclosures and start selling them at discounts below replacement costs. Watch for an increase in bank failures. These are indicators of fundamental opportunity and the start of a new base and renewal of market activity.

Understanding the Fundamentals of Land

Land is for holding. In some cultures, you just don't sell your land. I lean in that direction myself.

Buying land you can afford to keep and pay the carrying costs (interest and taxes) is likely to prove a safer and more secure investment than you can find in the popular financial markets.

At least you can put a good piece of land to use and grow crops or raise chickens and cattle. If you buy gold,

---

aside from worrying about theft, you have ownership of a nonproductive asset which may or may not prove to be useable as money.

Land is for building on. Aside from being a store of value, land supports construction of useful structures. When land is in the path of growth you can almost see the value increase.

A friend told me of a choice his father made many years ago. It was the selection of a location for a dairy. One was in a small town with little activity—a quiet life. The other was in a valley north of the state's largest and most active city, and not such a quiet life.

Operating a profitable dairy on land that is likely to be in demand as a city expands is not a bad way to earn while you wait. Unfortunately, my friend's father chose the quiet life, and the millions in land value for the north valley location went to others a few short years later.

Land is subject to the same market forces as any other form of real estate. Supply and demand rule, and a quiet town is less likely to generate the growth activity necessary to drive prices significantly higher.

Activity reflects growth and the supply and demand contest characteristic of real estate. Land activity is the first to be affected by a growing city moving beyond the edge of town.

Land subdivided for single-family lots is first in line for trouble when credit dries up or when housing supply saturates demand. Many a builder has lost the entire profit in a subdivision when demand ended and a large land inventory remained on the books.

Land serves many functions. It is a store of value. It is the source of productive activity, like farming. It is the foundation of residential housing for personal use and commercial property held for investment. Like other real estate, land can produce cash flow for you or require your cash flow. It is up to you to structure your investments to ensure a balance between the two.

Following the Third Law

1. Employment is the basis of population growth.

2. Demand for real estate follows population growth.

3. Supply is created in response to demand.

4. Credit can create demand, but it tends to distort normal market activity.

5. Areas of a city have a life cycle.

6. Older areas in a renewal cycle offer a good investment opportunity.

7. Monitor the fundamentals by staying in touch with real estate agents.

Chapter 4

The Fourth Law

Invest with the Cycle

Cycles are recurring fluctuations in market activity at regular time intervals. Investing with the cycle is nothing other than investing when it improves your position. The right action is the action (or inaction) that improves your position. You are on a path. That path has steps that go up and steps that go down. Your challenge is to know the difference.

So much of real estate, and investing in general, is learning to take steps that do nothing more than improve your previous position. It's not like you decide one day to invest in real estate and the next day you're financially secure with a stable income. That comes more gradually, as you improve your investment portfolio through the years.

The ebb and flow of supply and demand and credit combine with fear and greed to create real estate cycles. It is amazing how these ragged ups and downs of market activity fall into recurring patterns with regular timing tendencies. Cycles are historical records of human behavior. They are gifts with red flags, marking years in the future when we are likely to do it again.

Understanding the 7-Year Housing Cycle

Many of the characteristics of housing market activity are captured statistically by the government as part of its effort to measure the progress of our political economy. Housing starts, new home sales, and housing completions are reported monthly. Existing home sales are another favorite indicator for monitoring the resale market.

These market components reflect market activity, which is the sum total of buying and selling. Housing market activity tends to peak every 5 to 7 years. Some cycle peaks are obvious, such as the 2007 cycle. Some are barely noticeable, as occurred in the 2000 cycle. The reason for these differences often relates to the availability of credit at low rates.

Demand drives activity. Credit supports demand. Supply follows demand. This interrelationship is best seen in extremes. For example, the parabolic increase in prices during the low interest rate period of the late 1990s into the mid-2000s created demand in the extreme, to the point of a historically significant bubble.

During this period, greed overtook reason and everyone from mortgage brokers to bankers jumped on the easy-credit train. Money for housing loans was so plentiful that one of the biggest speculative booms in modern history consumed almost everyone involved in the real estate market.

Bankers had buyers for packaged home loans, so they spread the word that money was available for the taking. This may be the first time that money for home loans went looking for borrowers.

Usually, borrowers have to search for a good loan they can afford. During the housing boom of the 7-year cycle ending in 2007, however, fraud followed the money in an orgy of lax loan underwriting to create loans for people who couldn't begin to qualify under honest conditions.

You can imagine what this did to the supply of new homes as builders attempted to meet the frenzied demand. Land was bought and subdivided. Houses were built and sold; everybody touched by housing prospered for a while. Then the burden of bad loans caught up with a couple of the investment banks that went too far out on the limb of greed. When they collapsed, they set off a chain reaction from Wall Street to Washington, and across the nation and into Europe.

The combination of easy credit, fraudulent loans, and human folly all contributed to the misallocation of capital and an excess supply of houses. As always happens, the demand was eventually met, and the excess supply weighed on prices as buying and selling activity slowed, then stopped. Prices began to fall on a national level, surprising economists and the financial wizards — those same wizards who set up the securitization of home loans that greased the slide down.

This is the first time a drop in home prices was noticed nationally since the 1920s. Usually, we see regional and local price softening in response to periodic speculation and overbuilding and unemployment, but the 2007 peak was different. It was ignited by easy credit, fueled by intentionally-unenforced regulation, and then exploded as the gasoline of human greed spread across the country. The result was a national housing boom and bust, followed by a fraud-ridden credit collapse in 2008.

Timing the 7-Year Housing Cycle

The instructive thing about the 2007 peak is the way it clearly defined the components and participants in a speculative real estate boom and the tragedy of the bust that followed. The benefit of knowing and trusting timing tendencies of market activity is an appreciation of the consequences. This helps you choose the way you want to participate. By using cycles, which are both market history and warnings posted ahead in time, you have a distinct advantage.

There are many components to the housing market. Each peak is slightly different for each component. Housing starts, new home sales, home completions, housing permits, and existing home sales all have slightly different cycle timing within the 5- to 7-year topping process.

This is especially noticeable when so many people and market segments are involved in the extreme, as occurred in the mid-2000s. In prior peaks, one market component, such as existing home sales or housing completions, tended to come closest to the 7-year mark. The market peaked between 2005 and 2007 but this was not publicly acknowledged until the damage was well established in 2008. In the prior projected peak of 2000, market activity barely stopped to take a breath and kept on running up the hill of easy credit.

The key is to be aware of the investment decisions you make in the context of time. The time to invest is when the price and terms are right for you. However, there is always an advantage in knowing the timing of cycles.

Cycle fluctuations give you a negotiation advantage to get the best price and terms and provide awareness of when to buy and when to sell. They aid decisions but do not stand alone as the only criteria for buying and selling. Good buys exist at projected peaks and bad buys exist at projected troughs.

Here is the timing of the 7-year peak in the housing cycle:

Peaks: 1972, 1979, 1986, 1993, 2000, 2007, 2014, 2021, 2028, 2035, 2042, 2049

Watch the fundamentals of supply and demand and credit availability with an eye on likely cycle timing and you will have an advantage. Remember that it is not what you know; it's what you do with what you know that makes money. And most important, no one can predict the future with certainty. All we can do is project the past rhythms of history as tendencies for future human behavior.

The danger is in waiting for conditions to change and missing a specific investment. It is amazing how we keep going along, even under adverse market conditions. Work the market that you know regardless of the cycle. Just adjust your negotiation strategy and the price and terms to fit the cycle, but keep at it regardless of the general situation. Any time can be the right time if you structure the price and terms of an acquisition to fit your capacity to deal with the specific situation at hand.

Danger also resides in our unrelenting news media, which depends on daily tragedy and popular fear to sell air time, newsprint, and Internet pixels. What is happening outside your investment market may have little to do with your goal of financial security and stable income. But being overcome by the anxiety and promotion of insecurity that dominates today's news is not in anyone's best interest. Use it to your advantage—don't let it get to you. When things get bad, remember they always get better eventually.

Applying the 10-Year Financial Crisis Cycle

Cycles tend to be obvious in hindsight. Look at the drop in housing starts and then the drop in housing sales and completions and you can see the change in

---

quantities that comprise the housing cycle. Add a slowdown in existing home sales and the picture is usually clear. It is a process that can span more than one year and can form a trend as the years pass.

However, there are other cycles that affect the real estate and financial markets that can be more difficult to monitor. Recently, a 10-year cycle has surfaced, which may prove to be significant in years to come. So far, we have three reference points, each with increasingly dire consequences. It is the building intensity of these three prior occurrences that raises the yellow flag of caution in anticipation of this cycle's future.

For example, in 1987 the stock market crashed due to numerous technical factors. In 1997, the currency of Thailand collapsed, and an Asian currency crisis ensued, followed by a Russian bond default in 1998 and the failure of Long Term Capital Management in the U.S. In 2008, the subprime mortgage collapse hit the financial markets in the U.S. and Europe, bringing down housing prices and countless banks.

These financial panics always seem to have plenty of causes we can argue about. They may seem remote, but now the world is so interconnected with trade and finance that the causes can come from any direction and the effects can spread far and fast.

The good thing about looking at cycles is that we only focus on the probable time frame. Causes are for the high priests of finance to argue about—usually after the fact. Before the fact, the noted political economists seem cloaked by ritualistic denial and unable to recognize even the hint of developing danger.

Here is the 10-year financial crisis cycle timing:

1987, 1997-98, 2008, 2018, 2028, 2038, 2048, 2058

———

This cycle applies to real estate because the banks are still in trouble today and prone to bad trading judgment. Since credit can't be separated from housing and commercial real estate, financial crises will likely involve banks and continue to affect real estate, as occurred with the S&L crisis and the subprime loan crisis.

When the banks are in trouble, credit is in trouble. When credit is in trouble, real estate is in trouble. Congress seems incapable of dealing with the ongoing bank-credit-housing problems. So we must consider the conditions of the 2008 collapse as unresolved. Also, the scheduled housing cycle peak in 2014 will be four years old and on the down slope when the 2018 crisis is ready to hit.

Since nothing on Wall Street that might prevent another financial crisis has significantly changed, it is possible — and likely — that the next crisis will be more damaging. In contrast, a lot has changed on Main Street.

Although there has been progress, foreclosed houses that have not cleared the books of the banks still weigh on the market. High national unemployment and low wages continue to indicate the legacy of failed trickle-down economic-policy nonsense. And the government has probably done all it can get away with to bail out the financial sector while ignoring prosecution of the individuals who constructed the fraudulent house of cards for personal gain.

Ongoing conditions point to a serious cluster of cycle activity around 2018. Timing here could be another opportunity for favorable acquisition negotiation, especially when we look at the 18-year cycle of real estate activity.

Note also that 2018 is two years after the 2016

presidential election, which is likely to bring the usual political conflict and media-induced turmoil.

Watching the 18-Year Real Estate Cycle

When we add the 18-year real estate construction and investment cycle to the timing mix, the situation becomes even more revealing. This capital investment rhythm encompasses the general activity of investment and construction in the real estate market.

Credit availability and credit flows also appear to be a part of the 18-year cycle. Since real estate is credit dependent, there is every reason for credit to be a component here. And when we look at the timing of the latest trough in 2008, it is even easier to see the connection.

Financial crises carry messages. Cycles distribute these messages over time. And *The Great Continuing Contraction of 2008* was filled with messages and demonstrated the collision of three cycles.

The 7-year cycle peaked and was heading down on schedule in 2007 directly into the 10-year financial crisis cycle of 2008 just as the 18-year cycle was headed for a 2008 trough. All three hit in the same time frame.

Many people saw it coming despite the protestations of the powerful who always think they control the market. Delusion is popular these days. Even politicians panic when the fallout of a cycle crashes the political economy. Imagine the chaos in Washington if the next one is worse than 2008.

Here are the peaks and troughs of the 18.33-year cycle. Previously, I dropped the 0.33 for discussion ease, but now we are down to specifics so I am including the extra decimals.

Peaks: 1962.6, 1980.9, 1999.2, 2017.6, 2035.9

Troughs: 1971.8, 1990.1, 2008.4, 2026.7, 2045

Now we must watch for the events that might shed light on the conditions we could encounter in the 2017 to 2018 time frame that is mid-way through the 7-year housing cycle and at a peak in the 18-year cycle, in time for the 10-year financial-panic cycle. There are many things to keep an eye on. Watch the fundamentals.

In the meantime, relax; financial panic is for Wall Street and Washington, not for you. Try to live in the eye of the hurricane and keep calm in the knowledge that you have structured your circumstances so no matter what happens, it won't change your lifestyle.

There is always a danger of overreacting to the national chaos when locally, things are just fine. Keep your eye on your life and avoid getting caught in the web of worry spun by the media and sold by politicians who claim to want to keep you safe.

Financial independence and stable income from real estate go a long way toward providing a secure life that will support your ability to watch cycles go up and down without concern.

House prices may fall more on average, but will the price of your rental investment be affected? If you have positive cash flow from rent, low vacancy, and rapid equity buildup, what happens on the average and nationally—although important—may not affect you. What counts is what happens to you. You can structure your investment activity to make sure it's stable despite the troubles elsewhere.

Applying the Business Cycle to Real Estate

The business cycle is characterized by expansion to a peak followed by contraction to a trough. These periodic expansions and contractions in gross domestic product (GDP) occur, on average, about every 51 months. Their history goes back more than 150 years. It takes a committee of economists (the National Bureau of Economic Research) to determine when a contraction—called a recession—has started. Usually they make the determination several months into the recession.

The business cycle is a product of our political economy with participation by the Federal Reserve (Fed), usually by raising or lowering interest rates to prevent or precipitate a recession. When the Fed holds rates too low for too long, it tends to distort financial markets, leading to financial crises and severe recessions. This is in contrast to a common recession when the Fed is known to raise rates just when the economy is doing well. In both cases the Fed's stated objective is to avoid inflation or deflation, often with unintended consequences.

A typical recession involves a decrease in sales, a drawdown in inventories, and ultimately, a rise in unemployment and contraction in gross domestic product. This is a normal correction in preparation for a new economic expansion. Unemployed workers force recognition of the business cycle. Unemployment is not good for anyone, and the government goes to great effort to mute its effects. Unemployment is the primary risk to any business that depends on consumer purchasing.

But everyone needs a place to live. During *The Great Continuing Contraction of 2008*, as foreclosures increased, many people were forced by circumstances to move to apartments. Unemployment from the recession combined with over indebtedness from the housing boom, followed by the credit collapse and tight lending requirements froze many out of the single-family housing market.

Vacant houses and foreclosed homes hang over the market. Just as banks were loose and imprudent during the boom, they are restrictive and cautious in the aftermath. The pendulum swings from easy credit to no credit. This is fear and greed in action by the banks, demonstrating the human element of a cycle.

Interest rates are lower than ever before, but the cash to make the down payment and the income to pay the loan are hard to come by for many. And the psychological damage is even harder to overcome for those who lost their homes.

Given the trend of slow job growth and high unemployment, rental real estate is likely to gain a wide following and rents are likely to continue increasing. This will stimulate multifamily construction and the supply will increase.

The inside message of cycles is that nothing is forever, except that a new cycle will follow the previous one and a peak will follow the previous trough. There is no way to project future recessions, unless you consider the longer-term cycles and anticipate that they may coincide.

Here are the years in which recent recessions have occurred.

Recessions: 1970, 1974-75 1980, 1982, 1991, 2001, 2008-09

Recessions are slowdowns in business activity, as the political economy works off some sort of excess acquired during the previous expansion phase. They are attempts to bring housing, business inventories, credit availability, and other supply factors back in line with changes in demand. Recessions are supply-demand adjustments flowing naturally from market activity, but frequently in response to policy and regulatory action, changes in the law, and political conflict.

Negotiating within Cycles

Cycles are always with us. It's impossible to invest outside of a cycle. But it is possible to invest and not know you are at a cycle peak. Many have. Buying at the top in the frenzy of a boom is common. But you don't have to. It's also possible to shrink from the market at the trough out of fear, even though it is a favorable negotiation climate.

For example, an investor friend and I were coming back from a small town after being shown an apartment complex for sale. The broker who represented the seller asked if we were interested.

My investor friend and I had bought property together before. But this time we were in a serious recession at the bottom of a 7-year housing cycle and an 18-year real estate cycle trough. The property we were considering was poorly managed, neglected, and suffering from high vacancies, so he said he didn't want to get involved. But I jumped at the opportunity — it was the right property at the right time for me. From my vantage point, the price and terms were too good to pass up.

The negotiation was easy. The owner wanted out

from under this out-of-town property, even though the cash flow was covering expenses and debt service despite a high vacancy rate. I saw an opportunity for attentive management as the economy pulled out of the recession and the serious real estate slump.

For someone else, this would be property to avoid. The current owner didn't want it, and my investor friend didn't want the management burden. Not all negotiations come with this type of built-in ownership fatigue and cycle advantage. But it is important to recognize when such circumstances align to your advantage.

It is equally important to recognize the interests of the person sitting across the negotiation table. The reason this out-of-town property was easy to acquire was primarily because, unlike many owners, the interests of this owner were well defined and simple.

Negotiation is most effective when based on an understanding of the interests of the other party. If you don't fully grasp what is important to your counterparty, you will be at a distinct disadvantage. How can you explain the way your offer meets the interests of the other person when you don't have an insight as to what they are? The market cycle in force at the time is a backdrop to the negotiations, but the interests of the owner are specific and essential regardless of the phase of the cycle.

Your interests are essential as well, and the best transactions occur when both parties' interests are met. For example, in this transaction my interest was cash flow and the potential for increasing it. The seller's interest was elimination of the management demands of out-of-town property, which were easy for me to deal with, given the potential for cash flow from the apartments.

I was able to meet his interests by assuming the management and paying him with a portion of the existing cash flow. I met my interests by ensuring positive cash flow from day one, with the possibility of rent increases through attentive management. These apartments were not far from town. They met my criteria for access and made visits to the resident manager every three weeks or so feasible.

There is no doubt that the price and terms of this acquisition would not have been as favorable without the help of a falling set of real estate cycles. And without the help of the cycles, I could not have met my interests. In fact, I probably would have passed on the deal. I needed low payments on the second position paper carried by the seller to meet my cash flow goal. Cycles made it possible.

When the cycles are in a down trend, it is a favorable time for negotiation. Not necessarily because prices are falling, but because the psychological climate favors acquisition on terms beneficial for buyers. We were in a buyer's market and the position of the cycles made that clear. Five years later, we were in a seller's market and the cycles made that clear as well; so I sold.

Cycles demonstrate the unstable nature of our economy. They are gifts for the aware. Preparation for the next downturn should always be part of your thinking. This means you should get out of debt when times are good so your burden during the bad times is reduced. Raise your cash level during the expansion as the momentum of the economy builds. This may mean selling some property and it definitely means paying off any short term debt you have.

The lesson of cycles is to always be prepared for the

next phase — whether up or down; and arrange your life so no matter what happens, it will not change your lifestyle. And when the bottom hits, be ready to benefit from the coming move up.

Acquiring Land by Using Cycle Timing

Land is the treasury bond of real estate. In fact, today a well-positioned land investment may be safer than treasury bonds. It may also turn out to be better than gold. We'll see.

The purpose of investing for the long term is to transfer wealth through time while protecting it from inflation and deflation; that is, to preserve purchasing power. Wealthy families have always used land to ensure future generational wealth. For our purposes, the principle is just as valid.

You don't have to be ultra wealthy to benefit from adding land to your long-range plans. A base of rentals and an occasional purchase of a few acres in the path of growth make for a good mix of real estate. Land that can be farmed or leased for grazing is all the better.

A long-term investment in land is best made when the cycles are hitting a trough. Paying the lowest price possible is crucial for a profitable investment. Using cycles to your advantage is common sense. Invest when cash is in short supply and market psychology is filled with anxiety about the future.

Try to keep your purchase price low enough to absorb the carrying costs and still maintain a net positive appreciation over your anticipated holding period. Make your land investments based on the price, anticipated holding period, and likely appreciation.

Large tracts, farms, ranches, and timber land all

---

have potential for the transfer of intergenerational wealth. And when the time is right, after 50 or so years, selling a few hundred or thousand acres may place your adult grandchildren, who inherited the land, in the middle of more wealth than they could have imagined.

Following the Fourth Law

1. Cycles are part of our unstable political economy.
2. Knowing where we are in the cycle can give you an edge.
3. Try to buy when the cycle is at the bottom and starting to turn up.
4. Try to sell when buying is heated and the cycle is topping.
5. Watch for clusters of cycle extremes.
6. Use cycles as a backdrop for negotiation.
7. Don't be intimidated by cycle fluctuations — they help you.

Notes and References on Cycles

The 7-year housing cycle peak is drawn from my observation of the market components: New home completions tend to hit the 7-year mark with accuracy. Existing home sales come close. Building permits, housing starts and new home sales generally peak either side of the sixth year. Because of the intense efforts of the Federal Reserve to prop up the economy with low interest rates, the 2000 peak was barely noticeable, resulting in a distorted market followed by a 2007 peak and crash that were extreme and part of the general credit collapse.

The 18-year real estate activity cycle is a projection

---

of the work of Edward R. Dewey: The 18-Rhythm in *Cycles: Selected Writings* (Foundation for the Study of Cycles, 1970, p. 343). This cycle bottomed in 1990, following the savings and loan crisis, and moved into the topping phase in 1999 in time for the subprime mortgage crisis. The topping process extended into the early 2000s as the housing bubble expanded and burst, producing a crash into the 2008 trough. I discuss the detail of the causes in chapter 5 of my other book available at Amazon.com. *Real Estate Acquisition: 150 Techniques for Serious Investors*

The 10-year financial crisis cycle is a projection of a cycle from the first part of the nineteenth century as noted in *Manias, Panics and Crashes: A History of Financial Crises* (sixth edition, Kindleberger and Aliber 2011). This book is a classic and worth reading if you're interested in the history of our unstable political economy and how it really performs outside of the mythology of conventional economic teachings and media reporting. The 10-year cycle seems to have resurfaced from the 1800s, when financial panics occurred in 1816, 1826, 1837, and 1857.

If you are interested in following the details of our political economy unfold in real time, I suggest you read the financial blog that saw the bust coming and sounded the alarm in 2005: www.calculatedriskblog.com.

Chapter 5

The Fifth Law

Manage Your Property

Learning to manage your property is the direct way to financial security and a stable income. Take care of your property and it will take care of you. Add value for your customers, and your profit will grow. Your customers are tenants and the buyers of property you sell. The value you add to a property for them comes back to you as cash flow.

Management is a communication function. The way you interact with your tenants, subcontractors, and neighbors and how your property appears to the community reflect your management style and can have a direct effect on your income. Problems solved with professional skill, routine maintenance on a regular schedule, and capital improvements accomplished when first needed are all indications of good management—and good management is the single best way to protect your equity and the value of your property.

Managing Finances

Second to its communication function, management is applied accounting. Monitoring the rent coming in and the expenses going out is the simplest form of accounting. Routinely done and closely monitored, accounting gives you a handle on performance.

Accounting does not have to be overwhelming; it just has to be useful. For example, it is best to control those expenses that can be controlled. When you see a spike in the monthly water bill, chances are there is a leak. Leaking water faucets, sprinklers, or toilets leak more than water — they leak cash. Paying more than necessary for insurance is also a cash leak.

Cash leaks are not one-time expenses. They tend to flow through rental operations, robbing profit and diverting money from productive improvements. Money down the drain is money that cannot be applied to the reserve account or needed repairs that improve the appeal of your property to prospective tenants.

Things may seem to be going well, but when you realize the opportunity cost due to below optimum rental rates, something is out of kilter. Cash leaks are a clear loss of profit. The opportunity cost of below-optimum rent is more difficult to spot.

Achieving balance among expenses, maintenance requirements, capital improvements and the optimal rental rate is the challenge of management. The essential tool to meet this challenge is a good accounting system that allows you to monitor operations over time.

Monitoring cash flow starts with tracking rent payments, delinquencies, and late charges. It's true: sometimes tenants are late with rent. This is why care in tenant screening is good planning. Employment and income verification is best at all times.

Vacancies are the first drain on cash flow. Each month's vacancy is lost income that can never be recovered. Because it is such a final event, vacancy losses merit special effort.

Consider the rent you charge in relation to the market rate for similar rentals. Try to establish a competitive rate that provides real value for your tenants. Do everything possible to avoid prolonged vacancies.

For example, turnover is part of rental ownership. You can minimize losses from turnovers by finding a new tenant during the 30-day notice period provided by the tenant who is moving. This is the reason for requiring a 30-day notice to vacate. It gives you an opportunity to find a new tenant.

Operational expenses are the next source of cash flow leaks. Preventive maintenance pays in this area. Communication skills applied to maintenance contractors can also help reduce your costs. Shopping for competitive property insurance is prudent. Property taxes are difficult to control, but any increase should be matched against the tax on comparable properties and protested if the tax is inappropriate.

Capital improvements are too often overlooked or ignored. Surprises in this area are not pleasant. Reserves set aside from monthly rent are not a cash leak. Planning for capital improvements by placing an amount of your monthly rent in a reserve account is a sign of professional management.

Ensuring reserves for replacement of the roof, new appliances, kitchen remodeling, carpet, furnaces and air conditioning, and the unexpected, is good management practice. A separate banking account for this function is appropriate.

Ignoring ongoing replacement of needed items eventually shows in the rent you can charge. This is how the potential benefit of an improved property becomes a cash leak. The leak shows in the opportunity cost measured by lost rent and reduced property value due to deferred maintenance and capital improvements.

Here's a basic model for monitoring annual rental finances.

Potential income:
Less vacancy:
Equals income:

Less insurance:
Less maintenance:
Less municipal utilities and charges:
Less property tax:
Equals net operating income:

Less debt service:
Equals rental cash flow:

Isolating rental cash flow after vacancy, expenses, and debt service is the first step in deciding how much you should place in a separate reserve account for appliance replacement and capital improvements. A reserve account is not included in the monitoring of current operations because it is an investment account, which earns interest now on money to be invested in the future. It should be set up as cash flow permits and as indicated by future replacement requirements.

Negative rental cash flow emphasizes the importance of always having liquid funds for periodic cash requirements. Borrowing money for improvements is an alternative; when doing major improvements, it may be a better alternative. Going to a bank for a line of credit to improve property makes sense in many cases, especially when an increase in rent follows that will repay the loan.

Monitoring Remodeling

At some point, you may have to remodel or do extensive repairs. This is a different category than periodic painting, which may be the best way to maintain tenant appeal at a reasonable price.

A fixer upper that is easy to acquire and easy to add value to by remodeling can move you ahead fast. Doing the work yourself can save cash. Sweat equity is the foundation of investing when you don't have much money. With common sense and a willingness to learn, you can at least do your own cost analysis, get bids, and deal with subcontractors.

The key to a smooth project is clear communication with all involved. Written estimates and bids are essential. Change orders to the original contract must always be in writing to protect you and avoid misunderstanding. Anything involving money and work to be done in the future should always be written in some form and agreed to by all parties. Anything less is a request for surprises. Surprises involving money are best avoided.

Remodeling often costs more than new construction because you don't know what you will uncover. With new construction, you have an approved drawing that does not involve removing something to find a problem you couldn't have predicted. There are plenty of surprises with new construction, but they usually involve mistakes, delays, and cost overruns, not hidden and unforeseeable construction requirements.

For example, we were in the process of acquiring an older commercial building when in preparing to tear out the ceiling to increase the interior height of the space, one of the crew crawled into the rafters. He found about 10 buckets scattered strategically to catch rain leaks. We thought a new roof would be needed in the near future, but not as part of the initial remodeling.

Fortunately, this surprise was discovered during the inspection period and before closing. We were able to adjust the price to offset the cost of reroofing. Requiring disclosure of problems known to the seller should always be part of your negotiation and agreement. Even then, do a thorough inspection before closing to make sure the seller didn't forget something.

Remodeling always costs more than you expect. New construction always costs more than you expect. Adjust your expectations and get everything in writing, and you can move closer to avoiding serious cost overruns. No matter what, increase your budget by a certain reasonable percentage to take care of costs you can't foresee. Prepare for surprises in remodeling and you will be less surprised when they do surface.

Of course, if you don't have the money to hire a contractor to remodel your rental, doing it yourself little by little is not a bad alternative. You may find that you have a skill set that goes beyond fixing up old rentals. It could be you end up with your own contractor license.

One of the more successful apartment owners in our town started just that way. He found that getting his license and building his own apartment complexes worked better for him. His designs were unique, and by contracting the building he ensured quality and cost control. When he went to the bank for a loan, the hands-on insight and financial projections reassured the lenders and allowed him to establish a working relationship that lasted for years.

Maintaining Property

After acquisition and any initial remodeling, maintenance becomes the primary daily requirement. Experienced investors will tell you never to waste your time doing maintenance yourself. But when you first start to build a cash flow stream, you may want to save the hourly rates charged by repair professionals.

Finding a handyman service or a moonlighting jack of all trades who knows how to paint is an alternative that can free your time up to work on acquisition opportunities. If you don't have the time or skill or inclination, subcontracting for a repair service is an alternative. Cost control is always essential.

Randomly calling service companies every time a tenant has a leaking faucet is not the solution. Taking the time to find and establish a relationship with an individual who is skilled in general repair work is. You never know where a good working relationship will lead. Contacts come in many forms, and there is always someone who knows things you don't. Put the word out that you are looking for good deals in real estate, and your repairman may become a link in a chain of events that you could not have foreseen.

When I first started acquiring rentals, I discovered a neighbor who did repairs for others in the area. He was an older fellow who owned rentals, didn't have a formal education, but was intelligent and skilled in everything related to construction. He also knew people who owned property and a few who wanted to sell. It only took one contact and one acquisition for the helpful handyman to more than pay for his bill to me over the years. He was not interested in acquiring more. He owned enough. It seemed he enjoyed helping me get started, and I appreciated his help.

Relating to people is primary. Civility, respect and courtesy toward all are good rules to follow as you meet the challenge of managing property and as you make your way through life. Management is a social function that depends on communication. Maintaining your property is a subset of management driven by your relationship with tenants.

It is in your best interest to respond to your tenants' maintenance requests professionally. Turnover is money lost. Tenants are sources of cash flow. Maintaining a comfortable place for tenants to live or do business is a requirement for the stability of your income.

Dealing with Management Fatigue

Concern over the demands of management is a major reason many don't seriously consider investing in real estate. Management fatigue is a major reason rental property is offered for sale. If you are tired of the demands of ownership, there are solutions other than selling; but if you are acquiring property, the management fatigue of others can work in your favor.

When you first start investing, it is likely to take some time before you have a large enough portfolio to support hiring professional management. Fortunately, there are companies that manage property. The first step is to recognize that there is a time when turning management over to an established company is your best move.

Planning to place your property under professional management at a future time can allow you to move forward with your investment program. Not that you should plan to be tired of management, but it is useful to know that it is a common affliction you can deal with.

Here's the thing to keep in mind. People regret that they did not buy a certain property and they regret that they sold a certain property. They rarely regret that they own a property. Remember the four benefits of rental property and you will be reminding yourself why it makes sense to remain invested: Rental income; Appreciation; Tax shelter; Equity buildup.

Reducing your net operating income by paying a professional manager may be the only way you can retain the four benefits. It may seem attractive to book a profit by selling—but, ask yourself what you will forego by selling.

Real estate is a relatively illiquid, long-term investment. To realize the long-term benefits, you must stay invested. Five years after you sell, the cash you received will most likely be gone. If you don't sell, in five years you will still own the property and the four benefits it provides.

So consider professional management if you are suffering from management fatigue. It is better than regretting a premature sale and the loss of equity and all the long-term benefits that follow through the years to come.

Managing Ownership Risks

Environmental hazards are a fact of real estate life—you must deal with them. They can be expensive to remediate and a threat to the resale of your property. Former dry cleaning businesses and gas stations are frequently found to contain solvents or petroleum by-products that release fumes or contaminate the soil at their locations and the lots nearby.

An environmental study and soil testing of previously developed commercial property are necessary when you suspect environmental hazards in the area – not necessarily on the property itself. It is prudent risk control.

Owning real estate involves risk. It is part of investing. Dealing with the risks is part of management. There are risks associated with the fundamentals of supply and demand. There are risks associated with the credit markets and the ups and downs of the real estate cycles. And there are risks associated with the way you manage your property.

For example, it is important to follow the landlord-tenant laws of the state in which your property is located. This means learning the rules that apply to you and your tenants. It involves establishing a rental agreement or lease when you first rent that conforms to the law. Then you must deal with your tenants within the context of the rights and obligations you both have, as detailed by the law.

In some areas, protecting yourself means providing a degree of security for your tenants. Sufficient lighting along walkways and in parking lots, security cameras, and fencing all show a degree of awareness for the safety of your tenants. Neglect safety requirements at your own risk.

Insurance is mandatory. Certainly, fire and extended coverage are essential to protect your equity and are required by the mortgage holder. Beyond that basic coverage, increased liability protection or an umbrella policy might be worth considering, depending on your situation.

As your portfolio grows and your net worth

increases, your attorney may want you to consider putting each of your properties in a separate limited liability company (LLC). This would help isolate any claim related to one of your properties from the others. A judgment against one property would likely not attach to your other property or your personal holdings. Consult your attorney if you're concerned about the extension of liability to other assets.

Managing Land

Land is not management free. But it is relatively management free. In a sense, when you own land, you are the shepherd guiding the wealth it represents into the future for generations to follow. This may involve serious effort in the case of farm land, especially if you are the one doing the farming. It may involve simply paying the taxes and waiting for growth to catch up with your foresight if you own land in the path of growth.

The challenge of land acquisition is to make a choice that fits your plan and your time frame. This is a process of matching the land you buy with your expectations for it.

I was talking recently with a friend who had been searching for land on the Internet. He found several remote parcels that seemed cheap. He was interested because of the price, but wondered how he would develop such a lot. This particular subdivision had been sold out years before. A few houses were scattered around and there was electricity, but no water or sewer.

Obviously, he was looking for a way to make money from a lot that was a bargain by city standards, but he couldn't figure out why it was so cheap or how he could take advantage of the low price. The answer is in the fundamentals. Demand was nonexistent, and the lot was in the middle of a major over-supplied market area.

Taking advantage of seemingly inexpensive land is possible. The first step is to realize that the price has meaning only in the context of the supply-demand relationship. Looked at in this light, the lot he had in mind was very expensive.

There are two ways to make money in this situation: Get the price down and hold it for a long time, without expectation of profit any time soon. Time has to pass for the growth (demand) to move closer to the land (supply).

What does this have to do with management? Well, it is an example of how you can manage your own expectations in the context of a land investment that will take years to produce a profit. By understanding the fundamentals that determine price, you can adjust your expectations to fit the growth requirements necessary to make a profit.

And more directly, you are managing the timing of the land investment by purchasing at the price necessary to offset the risk of a long-term investment. Price adjusts the supply-demand relationship in the context of time only if you realize and require it.

Managing land involves more than adjusting your expectations to the supply-demand relationship and time. It also involves dealing with fire and water: making sure brush is controlled and drainage doesn't result in erosion. Fencing may also be necessary to prevent unintended easements from developing over time.

With land near the city limits, management can take a different and more proactive form. For example, bringing land into the city with favorable zoning can result in an immediate value increase. Property taxes will likely increase as well. So getting your land into the city with zoning is best done when you are planning to sell or develop.

Following the Fifth Law

1. Responsible management protects cash flow and equity.

2. Communication is essential to responsible management.

3. Maintain your property, and it will take care of you.

4. Add value for tenants and buyers, and your cash flow will increase.

5. Vacancy is a loss that can be managed.

6. Accounting is essential to managing cash flow.

7. Management fatigue can be controlled.

Chapter 6

The Sixth Law

Learn How to Exchange Real Estate

Exchanging real estate is essential if you want to maximize the growth of your portfolio. There are two reasons for this statement. First, exchanging is a way to use the property you own to acquire different property that improves your investment position. Second, in some cases, you can avoid paying capital gains tax on the disposition of your property by structuring an exchange.

Look at exchanging as an opportunity to increase the speed at which your investments grow. Treat it as a tool stored in the back of your mind, ready for use as you search for new investments. View equity as unrealized cash that is available for acquiring other property that will help you reach your investment objectives sooner.

Understanding the Benefits of Exchanging

Exchanging is primarily a way to increase the size of your real estate investment portfolio. As equity grows through acquisition and appreciation, it becomes a form of purchasing power that you can use in your acquisition strategy. Combined with the leverage of financing, exchanging can be a powerful and useful investment technique.

For example, a rental house can become the down

payment on a 20-unit apartment complex through exchange. This complex can become the down payment on 50-unit complex or a shopping center. Increasing the size of your portfolio is important because the inherent benefits of ownership expand. Rental income, appreciation, tax shelter, and equity buildup all increase in scale.

Rental income increases to a greater total when you raise the rent on a 20-unit complex by $5 dollars a month, compared to a rental house.

Appreciation in dollar amount on a 20-unit complex is greater than a rental house. Dollar appreciation is greater for the apartments because the appreciation rate (percentage) is applied to a larger property value.

Tax shelter may also be potentially greater because of the increase in depreciation of the larger complex.

Equity buildup will be larger because of the larger loan on the 20-unit apartment complex.

Exchanging to build your portfolio makes sense in so many ways, even before consideration of the tax savings. In some cases, tax savings are secondary to the investment and business reasons to exchange.

Focusing too much effort on avoiding tax liability can result in misplaced analysis emphasis. Getting into an investment that is not right for you because the negative attributes are offset by tax savings is never a good idea.

Structuring Exchanges

Exchanges are usually structured as either a two-way or multiparty transaction.

The two-way exchange involves two properties. Consider two houses of equal value with no debt. Each owner wants the other's house, so they trade. Rare, but it happens.

For example, a builder renovated and lived in an old house not far from where I live. Due to an unpleasant legal run-in with a neighbor, he decided to move. As fate would have it, he found another older house on 5 acres owned by a widow who wasn't interested in dealing with maintenance.

Equities in the two properties were roughly equal. Builder and widow exchanged, motivated by circumstances they both wanted to avoid, but ending with circumstances that greatly improved their lives. Tax consequences were not a consideration.

One went from maintenance problems to a virtually new home and the other went from neighbor conflict to five acres he could subdivide and build on. Neither party wanted the property they owned. Or, more accurately, neither wanted the problems associated with the property they owned. One party's problem was the other's solution. That is the central principle of exchanging.

Multiparty exchanges involve three parties. Usually, one wants an exchange to avoid tax (the exchanger), one wants to sell for cash (the seller), and one wants to buy (the buyer). The problem for each becomes the solution for the other.

It is not easy to find an owner to exchange with who also wants your property. Finding a buyer is more likely. But since you want to avoid capital gains tax, finding replacement property owned by a willing seller is a must.

For example, an investor found a prime commercial center that was about to be offered on the open market. The seller was leaving town and wanted to cash out. This active investor owned an apartment complex that he wanted to exchange tax free. The only thing missing was a buyer for the apartments.

To structure the transaction, the investor-exchanger and the commercial center seller entered into an agreement that was contingent on the exchanger finding a buyer for the apartments within a certain time period. And most important, it required that the cash for the apartments go to the commercial center owner. The exchanger had no access to, or constructive (contractual) or actual right to, the cash.

All exchange structures depend on properly written agreements by competent and knowledgeable attorneys. Here, the agreement legally restricted the exchanger's right to receive cash from the sale of the apartments: the cash went directly to the commercial center seller; the title to the center went directly to the exchanger-investor; the apartments were deeded directly to the buyer by the exchanger. The entire transaction was in one escrow, with all properties closing at the same time.

One party's problem was another's solution. The time provided by the exchange agreement allowed the solutions to unfold. So far, we have discussed a two-party exchange and a multiparty exchange in which property for exchange is in sight. Now, we will look at a more common multiparty sequence.

In this variation of the multiparty exchange, the buyer approaches the exchanger to sell, but the exchanger refuses because of the tax liability.

The buyer and exchanger agree to exchange if the buyer finds replacement property acceptable to the exchanger, buys it, and completes the exchange.

For example, a rancher was approached to sell property that had been in his family for generations.

Because of the significant capital gains tax due on sale, he suggested that the buyer locate and purchase income property for an exchange. In the prior multiparty exchange, the replacement property was found before the buyer. In this transaction, the buyer arrives before the replacement property.

To structure this exchange, the buyer and exchanger-rancher enter into an agreement that requires the buyer to locate replacement property and make an exchange. In practice, the exchanger will actually locate the replacement property and the buyer will agree to acquire it in writing, contingent on the exchange. At closing, the cash goes to the replacement-property seller; the replacement property goes to the exchanger; and the buyer gets the ranch. Closing occurs out of one escrow, with all properties closing at the same time, under the contingencies of the exchange agreement.

So far, we have discussed three types of exchanges:

1. Two-way exchange. The owners want each other's property more than they want the property they have.

2. Multiparty exchange with replacement property located. The exchanger has found property he wants, but the seller wants cash; so a buyer is found for the exchanger's original property.

3. Multiparty exchange with a buyer located. A buyer approaches the exchanger, who does not want cash; so replacement property is located that the buyer purchases and exchanges with the exchanger.

In each of these structures, the exchange agreement governs and controls the rights and obligations of the parties involved. Property is deeded directly to the ultimate owner, and in the multiparty exchange structures the cash goes to the seller without passing through the exchanger.

Most real estate exchanges are variations on the three types above. For example, multiple exchanges can involve several owners and properties. Any one participant may be selling or buying or giving and receiving real estate, depending on individual circumstances.

Any combination of investment objectives can be seen in a multiparty exchange. Ultimately, there are three primary variables: people, property, and money. In these structures, the transactions are contingent on the others closing. Consequently, they close out of escrow at relatively the same time, provided all the contingencies are met.

Market experience has shown that closing multiple properties at the same time is not always a realistic expectation. Human ingenuity, as usual, has found the solution in the form of a defined time delay.

Understanding the Deferred Exchange

Currently, the most common exchange structure is number three above, with a time delay. In active real estate markets, demand pushes against supply, and buyers come out of the woodwork. Property that will satisfy an owner who wants to exchange is difficult to locate. Buyers want ownership now, they have cash and they will move on unless accommodated. Owners want the right property in exchange and won't move forward until it is located.

Fortunately, the deferred exchange meets the

demands of the market while protecting the tax advantages. In a deferred exchange, the exchanger deeds to the buyer, but has no right to the cash for the property. The cash is held by an unrelated third-party facilitator for the sole purpose of acquiring replacement property. Consequently, the buyer gets the property and the exchanger gets time.

For example, the owner of a small hotel was approached to sell at a price he could not refuse. Because he had owned this property for many years, his capital gain was large; paying capital gains tax would significantly reduce the reinvestment proceeds. He wanted an exchange and the buyer agreed, provided he received ownership as soon as possible without waiting to find exchange property.

To preserve this top-dollar sale, the hotel owner (exchanger) and the buyer entered into an exchange agreement, with a title company acting as a qualified intermediary. The agreement provided for the transfer of the hotel to the buyer within 30 days and the holding of the cash in trust solely for future purchase of exchange property. Within 45 days from transfer of the hotel the exchanger found three potential properties, which were formally designated by letter as potential replacement properties.

The exchanger then negotiated the favorable acquisition of a self-storage complex that was on his designated property list. He signed an agreement to purchase, which was assigned to the buyer, subject to, and contingent on the exchange agreement with the title-company intermediary. At closing, the title company paid the money from the hotel sale to the seller of the self-storage complex, who deeded ownership of the complex to the exchanger (former hotel owner). The exchange closed within 180 days of the initial transfer of the hotel to the buyer.

It is important to note that the title company was a party to the exchange agreement, acting as trustee-facilitator for purposes of the exchange. This was not just an ordinary escrow function. The rights and obligations of the title company as trustee were defined in detail by the exchange agreement it signed with the exchanger and the buyer of the hotel. An ordinary title-company escrow does not protect the tax benefits of the exchanger.

There are benefits to exchanging real estate that go beyond the tax savings. It is all too easy to lose sight of the many reasons to exchange when only focused on the maze of requirements for protecting the tax-free status.

The tax savings of an exchange should be routine and the result of well-crafted documentation by a competent attorney. In fact, the tax benefit can sometimes be small, if the realized gain and tax rates are low, and should always be calculated before signing an agreement.

Applying the Investment Benefits of Exchanging

Admittedly, in today's investment world, it is difficult to separate the value of an investment from the value of its tax savings. Both are cash flows to you. However, losing sight of investment benefits because you are blinded by the light of saving a dollar on taxes is risky. It is usually more useful in the long run to acquire property because it makes investment sense, not because of tax considerations.

The following is a list of the primary investment and business reasons for exchanging without consideration of the tax benefits. When you know the underlying investment reasons to exchange you can open your mind to opportunities that may have been missed before. The tax savings are valuable, but try to place them in a secondary position because they can change at the whim of government.

1. Increase the size of your real estate portfolio by exchanging up in total value, using the equity you have from appreciation and equity buildup.

2. Exchange for management-free property or property that can support professional management.

3. Acquire property without cash by exchanging for property that requires only property and notes to balance values.

4. Exchange for property that you can borrow against and get tax-free cash by refinancing after, and independently of the exchange.

5. Exchange for property that is appreciating faster than the property transferred.

6. Exchange land for rental property to increase cash flow.

7. Consolidate properties by exchanging several smaller properties for a single larger property of equal value.

8. Relocate or expand to a different geographic location by exchanging.

9. Automatically solve the problem of where to invest by arranging an exchange rather than a one-property sale.

10. Diversify and spread investment risk by exchanging for several properties.

At its core, exchanging is a process of changing ownership circumstances. During periods of high taxation, saving the cash that would otherwise be paid in tax can be equally important.

Isolating the Tax Benefits of Exchanging

Tax savings are important. A low basis from years of depreciation taken on rapidly appreciating property, can make an exchange mandatory. If your capital gain is large enough that the tax will hurt, it is best to arrange an exchange. Here are the basic tax reasons to exchange.

1. Conserve equity by not paying tax on realized gain.
2. Increase depreciable basis by acquiring larger property encumbered with larger debt.
3. Acquire sheltered income by exchanging unimproved land for improved rental property.
4. Reallocate basis by acquiring property with a higher building-to-land ratio.
5. Conserve an estate by exchanging throughout life without loss of appreciated value to tax.

There are plenty of reasons to work exchanging into your investment planning and none of them will bore you. Preserving the hard-won equity of your property from taxation as you expand your investment holdings is reason enough. But the investment objective should always lead the tax-savings objective.

Understanding the Basic Tax Rules of Exchanging

Section 1031 of the Internal Revenue Code (IRC) provides that property held for use in trade or business, or for investment, may be exchanged for property of like kind. This rule has two components.

1. Use of the property: Under Section 1031 you can only trade property used in business or for investment—not your residence or property held for sale.

2. Like-kind property: This refers to the distinction between real and personal property. Real property, as defined by state law, can be traded for real property. Personal property can be exchanged for personal property.

Simple enough, but too often these distinctions are lost and lumped together as the like-kind requirement. It is important to keep them separate in your thinking to avoid mistakes and missed opportunities.

The use requirement means that property held for investment or use in business may be exchanged for property used in a business or for other investment property—each for each, or the other for the other. Property used as a personal residence falls under different and more lenient rules; it does not meet the held-for-investment or business-use requirement. Property held for sale in the course of business—such as a builder's lots—does not qualify.

Like kind includes the bundle of rights of real estate—not just land and buildings. This means that leases of 30 or more years, mineral rights, water rights, and all the other rights considered real property under state law may be exchanged for each other without tax liability.

Each type of real property may be exchanged for any other type. A leasehold interest with 30 years to run may be exchanged for a ranch, and mineral rights may be exchanged for an apartment complex. "Flexibility" and "accommodation" describe the history of exchanging. New applications are being clarified yearly as court cases are decided and revenue rulings are issued.

Personal property can play a role in a real estate exchange. For example, a furnished apartment complex will have a certain part of its value allocated to furnishings. Furniture can qualify if it is exchanged for other personal property as part of a real estate exchange. Keep this in mind to avoid surprises.

Defining Boot

"Boot" is anything of value in an exchange that does not meet the use requirement or is not like-kind property — anything taxable.

The history of modern exchanging has its roots in the west and rural areas where farm land and ranches are the currency of trading. This is likely the source of the word "boot", describing the process of kicking the trade to completion by adding a little additional consideration "to boot."

Few exchanges involve property with equities that just happen to balance. Consequently, boot is often added to make the deal.

Financing is also used to balance equities. One party may create a second loan secured by the relinquished property to avoid receiving cash. However, a note not secured by the property is boot and is taxed based on its fair market value.

Mortgage relief is a hidden form of boot to guard against. Reduction in loan liability is treated as boot. An exchanger who assumes a loan on the replacement property smaller than the loan on the relinquished property is subject to taxation on the difference, up to the amount of realized gain on the relinquished property.

For example, if the replacement property has a loan

---

of $300,000 and the relinquished property has a loan of $500,000, there is a danger that $200,000 will be subject to tax up to the amount of the realized gain on the relinquished property.

In an exchange, if you receive cash, property that is not like-kind, mortgage relief, or any other form of boot, you will be subject to tax on the value to the extent you have realized gain in the relinquished property.

Realized gain of $100,000 and boot of $10,000 results in recognized gain of $10,000, which is subject to capital gain tax rates. Realized gain is the difference between your market value and your adjusted basis in the property. Recognized gain is the portion of realized gain that is taxable. An exchange can be partially taxable. All of this is good reason to hire a competent accountant. See *IRS Publication 544* for more detail.

Balancing Equities in an Exchange

Balancing equities is the key to a successful exchange. It is how both parties receive equal value. Equity is the difference between the market value of a property and the loan on the property.

For example, a $900,000 property with a $200,000 loan has equity of $700,000.

Market value: $900,000
Less loan: $200,000
Equals equity: $700,000

If you want to exchange this property for one valued at $4 million, with a loan of $3 million, you must offset the $300,000 difference to balance the equities.

Market value: $4,000,000
Less loan: $3,000,000
Equals equity: $1,000,000

Replacement equity: $1,000,000
Relinquished equity: $700,000
Difference: ($300,000)
Boot given: $300,000
Balance: 0

In this example, you are exchanging for a larger market value, loan, and equity. Consequently, you are giving boot in some form rather than receiving it and, as a result, you probably have a tax-free exchange. This difference, which you are balancing with boot, may in fact be a second mortgage on the replacement property, not cash. There are many ways to balance equities.

Be careful not to confuse the process of determining realized gain with the process of calculating equity. They are completely separate and unrelated calculations.

Realized gain is the difference between exchange value and adjusted basis. Equity is the difference between market value and the loans on the property. Realized gain is a tax calculation that is determined in order to specify your tax liability without an exchange. Equity is an investment calculation that is determined as part of the process of balancing equities.

Exchanging Land

Land is where real estate starts. It is no different when land enters an exchange.

Once I met a rancher who was a member of a pioneer family that had acquired land and ranches throughout the Southwest. He owned a business in the Midwest, but kept the family tradition of trading and acquiring land going. He drove a pickup powered by propane and visited his property and ranching contacts regularly.

His exchange and acquisition strategy was simple: stay in contact with as many land owners as possible; eventually one will want to trade or sell. He learned this simple secret the hard way.

Before I met him, he decided that flying to his property in a Cessna 180, the pickup of the sky, was a good idea. It would save time and allow him to cover more territory to deal with his wide-spread management responsibilities. It took about a year before he realized the mistake he had made.

This rancher noticed that he wasn't making the number of trades or acquiring the property that was typical during a year. Flying over the West seemed to have removed him from the action. He was moving faster but not staying in contact with the ranching community. Once the evidence was in, he parked the plane and started driving again.

Parking the Cessna soon resulted in a multiparty exchange involving a ranch traded for a shopping center on a land lease with 35 years to run. The rancher was the ranch buyer in the multiparty exchange. The ranch owner was the exchanger who got the shopping center on a land lease and the shopping center owner got cash.

This is an illustration of how land can be exchanged for a leasehold interest with 30 or more years to run without tax. It is important to remember that the bundle of real estate rights includes many components, each of which can be exchanged for the other.

Acquiring fast-appreciating land in the path of

growth and exchanging it a few years later for income-producing property is a cash-flow strategy that has worked for many years.

Following the Sixth Law

1. Exchanging is a process of improving your investment position.

2. The tax benefits of exchanging vary based on tax rates and property basis.

3. Like kind refers to real property as distinguished from personal property.

4. There are many ways to balance equities in an exchange.

5. An exchange can be partially taxable and still qualify under the tax code.

6. A deferred exchange solves the time delay for a buyer.

7. Exchanging can build your portfolio without equity lost to tax.

Chapter 7

The Seventh Law

Always Own Some Real Estate

Real estate connects you to the earth. No matter how good or how bad life may be, always keep some real estate and you will have stability. Maybe a plot of land in a good location or a rental house will be your fall-back position if you hit rough going. No matter what happens, hold on to some real estate.

I have heard many people lament that they sold property. Few complain about buying property. This does not mean there is no one with buyer's remorse. Certain acquisitions can turn out to be problem property, but usually a solution can be found. Owning some real estate holds the potential of a rewarding outcome in the future. If you let go of all your property, you lose that potential — that hope for the future.

Making Money When You Buy

One of the tenets of investing is that you make your money when you buy — not when you sell. Buy at the wrong time or price, and it can be a struggle to make a profit, and a long wait for the market to catch up to you.

It just increases your risk to buy at the wrong time in the cycle, or at the wrong price.

If you realize that your profit in the future depends on the price you pay today, negotiations can be intensified and risks can be minimized.

Liquidity in real estate is a function of price. The lower the price, the easier it is to sell property because there is always someone in the market who realizes that you make your money when you buy. And at the right (low) price, that person will step up fast. This is why cash is so important when the real estate cycle is in a down trend.

Risk can be controlled more easily when care is taken at the time you acquire property. Price and financing both contribute to risk control. The cost of ownership has many components. Some are known and some are unexpected.

For example, a land investment with no income and a long holding period should be analyzed by adding the property taxes and loan interest paid during ownership. Try to anticipate all the cash flows that go into holding the property and compare them with the cash flows you expect will come from the property—it is the net that you get.

Real estate investment is not for everyone. People get tired of managing property and the demands of ownership. Some people find that they are not suited for it. Some don't want to be bothered. Some don't have the management-ownership personality trait. Many don't realize any of this until after they buy and experience what is involved.

Sellers who can't resolve the normal problems of real estate ownership are among the most cooperative and easy to negotiate with. Owners who are selling because they don't want to deal with problems present an unique buying opportunity.

When you buy problems, you provide a service to the seller—relief that qualifies for special consideration.

If you can see the solution, and price in a discount that is appropriate, you move closer to making a profit when you sell.

Every small step you take toward reducing your initial cost is an adjustment in risk. The price you pay is the obvious place to start. It is the foundation of the money you make when you sell.

Trading Capital for Cash Flows

Investment is a claim on future cash flows. You measure the return represented by the cash flows you pay by comparing them to the discounted cash flows you receive. This measurement process can be an ongoing projection of likelihood or done when you sell and the total of the cash coming in and the cash going out is known.

When you buy, you set the first benchmark for determining the return you will receive. That's why the price you pay is crucial to minimizing risk and maximizing profit. For example, buying below the market price captures immediate value. This is appreciation by negotiation. Raising rents that the former owner held below the market captures additional rental income, which may justify a higher appraisal. Refinancing based on a higher appraisal might mean additional cash flow to you, especially if it allows you to pay off a second-position private loan at a discount.

When you invest, you trade capital for cash flows. To make a good trade, you must take care to determine if the cash flows you expect are likely to occur. This is the risk you expose your capital to in any investment. Your investment capital is equity in property. It returns to you through future cash flows.

For example, a $25,000 down payment that produces the following cash flows from multiple benefits illustrates the trade of capital for cash flows.

Net Cash Flows:

Year 1 rents: $2,000

Year 2 rents: $2,300

Year 3 rents: $2,500

Year 4 rents: $2,500

Year 5 rents: $3,000

Year 6 refinance proceeds: $10,000

Year 6 rents: $3,000

Year 7 sale: $50,000

Total cash flows: $75,300

This cash flow stream would make sense to most investors *(IRR, 18.32%)*. The challenge is that, when you commit $25,000 you take the risk that comes with not being able to know future performance. That's why the purchase price is so important to any investment. You just don't know for sure what the future holds, and that reality must somehow be taken into consideration in the price you pay and the liability you assume.

Equity protection is the primary objective. It starts when you negotiate the initial acquisition and continues through ownership.

Everything you do that contributes to protecting your equity will likely contribute to your cash flows. Your down payment becomes your equity. Your equity becomes your cash flows. It's a dynamic trade of capital for cash flows.

When you acquire property and the seller agrees to carry back a portion of the equity on a second position, you have an opportunity to negotiate certain advantages.

It is even better if the seller is privately financing the entire purchase. Seller-financed acquisitions don't necessarily involve the restrictions of a bank's loan committee. You're dealing with fewer decision makers, so the likelihood of negotiating flexible terms is greater.

For example, there are elements of a loan that work to your advantage during ownership and when you sell. High leverage with little or nothing down is a good place to start. A very low interest rate and interest-only payments for a certain period of time add flexibility. No personal liability on an assumable-nonrecourse loan makes a good combination in anticipation of a sale in a few years. With a land purchase, release clauses that provide for transfer of a portion of the property to you as the loan is paid down can add to your equity and cash flow protection and reduce your risk of loss.

Everything you can think of that protects the capital you're trading for cash flows is important and should be worked into the agreement when feasible.

Getting Money When You Sell

When you sell, you trade cash flows for capital and the circle is complete.

Exchanging for other property and carrying private financing when you sell are the exceptions. Exchanging is the method of choice if you plan to maintain your capital investment in real estate. Here, you're replacing capital with different capital and cash flows with different cash flows, all without converting equity to cash. This is why an exchange can be nontaxable.

When you get an appraisal, the value will likely be determined based on one or more of three standard appraisal approaches. Each has its merits, and combined they can produce a reasonably comfortable snapshot of the property's market value.

1. Cost approach: value based on replacement costs of building and land.

2. Comparable sales approach: value based on sales prices of comparable properties.

3. Income approach: value based on capitalized (or discounted) rental income.

The appraisal process brings the importance of good management into focus. This is where an experienced professional evaluates the work product of your ownership efforts.

However, certain aspects are not in your control. For example, you have no control over the price of land and building costs used in the cost approach.

You have no control over the comparable sales of other properties. But you do have a hand in the condition of the property and the rental rates you are charging, within the limits of the market.

Well cared-for and responsibly managed property shows the effort—especially to an appraiser. This effort will translate to money when you're trying to maximize the amount you get from a sale.

More than anything else, the relationship between rental income and the expenses required to operate the property determines the value to the new buyer, just as it did when you bought.

Net operating income, capitalized based on similar properties, is most important in an investment appraisal. The capitalization rate of similar sales in your area will be applied to your property to estimate its market value.

For example, if your annual net operating income is $53,000 and properties in your market area are selling based on a capitalization rate of about 7 percent, your property will likely be valued at around $757,000 based on the income approach ($53,000 / 0.07 = $757,143).

The comparable sales approach examines similar properties and converts their sales prices to values per square foot so they can be compared. For example, if you're selling 20 acres for development and the range of sales for similar property is $1.55 to $1.65 per square foot, you have an idea of what to ask when you sell and what it might appraise for.

There are 43,560 square feet in an acre, so 20 acres valued at $1.60 per square foot yields $1,393,920: (20 x 43,560sf = 871,200sf) and (871,200sf x $1.60 = $1,393,920).

Measurement by square foot is central to real estate. We determine the size of a house by using square footage and we refer to prices of city land by square footage. This allows comparison of any type or size of real estate on the same measurement basis.

For example, when using the cost approach an appraiser determines the cost per square foot to buy land and replace a commercial building. In some cases, this might involve adjusting a building value for age and condition, and consequently, the value per square foot. Learning to think in terms of square footage is basic to understanding the language of real estate and how it is valued for sale.

Being in the Market

There is no substitute for being there. The more time you can spend on real estate, the more you'll learn. The more you learn, the greater your advantage. The greater your advantage, the more you'll be able to apply personal initiative to ensure your financial security.

If there was ever a time to take control of your

financial future, it's now. Developing skills that don't depend on corporate or government employment is more important than ever. Real estate investment in a local market that you are comfortable with is a good start.

Self-reliance and knowledge of your local real estate market are increasingly important to financial security. Invest locally in real estate that you know. Watch it carefully. And be patient.

Allowing the time necessary for opportunities to develop is difficult. Seeing them when they arrive requires care. Holding onto them is a challenge. Being in the market is essential. Finding good opportunities takes persistence. Developing a sense of opportunity when it arrives takes a little experience and a willingness to take action and make a few mistakes during the learning process.

You might be talking with a friend or a real estate broker and in the back of your mind, you think, "Pay attention, this could develop into something significant."

During a conversation, while you are listening, you may become aware that you're learning of an opportunity that is worth pursuing. Maybe the person you're talking with has the inside track on property coming onto the market. Maybe there's a cash buyer for property you want to sell. So you listen. Stay quiet. Learn. All you know at this point is to be alert. What is happening at this moment could be important to your future security.

Then you take the next step. Drive by the property. Meet with the people involved, or their agents. Opportunities unfold at their own pace because the people involved work at their own pace. When you sense opportunity, you can move into the flow of events, becoming part of the process, influencing where you can, working to align the variables to meet your personal interests. This is what being in the market means.

Staying Informed

We are in the middle of huge changes in the world of finance and real estate. Our demographics are changing as the boomers born after WWII begin to retire. This process is removing a large segment of the consumer economy from the work force. You might think this would open jobs for the next generation.

But many of our manufacturing jobs have moved overseas under the guise of opening markets to free trade and the challenge of competition. The backbone of our economy and source of our jobs — corporations — have moved entire plants out of the country in search of cheap labor and increased shareholder value. This is how we compete to our own detriment, as wages drop while corporate profits grow. The minimum wage today would have to be at $10 an hour just to reach the 1968 inflation-adjusted amount.

Strains are growing in the retirement system as businesses actively exit the liability of providing pensions to retirees. Concurrently, there is a political movement to reduce the obligation of the federal government to maintain Social Security and Medicare. Cities are going bankrupt under the demands of public employee retirement payments, negotiated over years by unions and generous local politicians. Public schools and universities face the same dilemma. The reality of compound growth has caught up with the generous negotiators of the past who did not understand the implications of exponential growth and the rule of 72.

These developing trends are loud warnings for young people. Jobs are hard to find. The benefits of health insurance and employer retirement contributions seem to be evaporating from all but the most generous businesses and government programs. Always owning some real estate takes on personal importance under these conditions.

Part-time employment is in favor as businesses attempt to avoid the cost of providing health insurance. Retirement saving relies on individual retirement accounts and the responsibility of each person alone, with no guarantee of success.

Low interest rates paid by safe-investment treasury securities seem normal now, out of necessity. An increase would balloon the costs of the federal government. Low safe interest rates place pension funds in grave danger of not meeting their actuarial requirements. State and municipal employment promises are testing the limits of exponential growth with retirement plans that can't begin to match their pension commitments from investment or tax revenue.

Risk-free investment in government bonds for a reasonable interest rate is a distant memory. Investment and business cycles are becoming more volatile just when the average citizen is being handed personal responsibility for retirement funding. These circumstances challenge the best-trained investment advisors and move lone individuals into the realm of finance — whether they like it or not at a time when confidence in our financial leaders is at a historical low.

It is easy to understand why investment real estate is growing in popularity. Local real estate, where you can exercise a degree of personal control and knowledge, is a refuge from today's volatile political economy. It is a relatively safe harbor where you can gain a degree of control over your financial future. Where else can you walk into your own back yard and see a rental house in the distance that is steadily building a savings account with deposits made monthly by a renter who is also your neighbor? This is investing in your own back yard in an area you know well.

Part of staying informed is knowing the investment choices available, and the relative risk of each. Determine where you feel comfortable enough to take action: start investing, acquiring, or trading, while keeping your goals of financial security and stable income clearly in mind.

Thinking for Yourself

Investing always requires taking responsibility for your decisions — at least it should. If not you, who? Some people would like to turn the burden over to an advisor — and do. There are benefits to getting professional advice and different perspectives. But you have to live with your decisions and learn from them. When you follow the advice of a financial advisor, it is still your decision and your responsibility. Trying to shift responsibility to another person who may be just drifting through your investment life is not in your best interests.

Self-reliance is part of the foundation of financial security; when you are aware of its importance, your confidence is likely to increase. Eventually, you will develop an instinct for investment pursuits that fit your skill and emotional capacity. Any anxiety you may have felt when you started will become hard to remember, replaced by understanding and knowledge. When that time arrives, you will have accomplished something that is as important as any perception of financial security you may have.

Professionals in specialized fields have access to information and direct contact with market developments that exceed what is available to lone individuals. Finding a real estate agent you can work with will give you an inside track. If you find one who is skilled in negotiation, with a knack for getting transactions through closing, you will have a valuable resource for years of successful investing.

An effective attorney is also essential to your progress. Find an attorney who specializes in real estate. Look for a problem solver who will work on your behalf to improve your position by helping you push the transactions through closing while protecting you legally. Avoid those who obstruct and are negative, time-consuming contract correctors. Find a facilitating lawyer who enjoys the law.

Complexity rules with tax requirements. They change with the winds of Congress and grow in volume year by year. An accountant is a must for real estate tax reporting. Unless you have specialized knowledge and interest, find a good accountant to save time and reduce the chance of errors.

Thinking for yourself does not mean you should avoid seeking professional help. It means realizing when you do need help and taking action to get it. Communicate clearly and make sure the professionals you choose understand your purpose. Remember that management is communication and you have the responsibility to manage the professionals who work with you. They have specialized knowledge, but you have the responsibility for the outcome.

Critical thinking is a tool. It should be automatic and

ever-present as you move through the years of your investment life. Be especially alert during times of easy money. This is when people become too trusting and subject to sales pitches for investments that make sense only in their imagination, but never in the real estate market.

Usually, this fraud is sold over the years as a cycle peaks. It characteristically takes the form of a financial instrument, such as a note couched as a loan, paying interest way above market rates. The schemer then uses the income from new "investors" to pay interest to earlier ones. When you understand compound growth, it is easy to see that this type of Ponzi scheme always has an unhappy ending.

Real estate is often involved in some way. Notes are often sold with the promise that the funds will be invested in the booming real estate market. The "greater fool" theory of flipping over-priced property by one fool to a greater fool is part of the normal real estate cycle and history of finance. Selling notes as loans to invest in real estate illustrates how debt and equity are locked hand in hand, even as they walk into the fog of fraud.

Always keep a skeptical eye open. Trust what you know to be true, not what you want to be true. Apply your math skills to see if the words you hear pass the test of objective reality. Strive to analyze and validate your own personal observations.

Avoid the trap of believing that you know what the future holds, but never pass up the chance to make an educated analysis. Divide your expectations into three categories:
1. Pessimistic
2. Most likely
3. Optimistic

Work toward thinking in terms of probability. Avoid certainty and any tendency to convince yourself you have the gift of foresight. It only leads to being constantly surprised — usually not in a good way.

Protecting Against Our Unstable Political Economy

Our political economy continues to prove that it is inherently unstable. This is not a new discovery. The rush for money and speculative gain is part of our real estate and investment history. Banks are central to this volatile process because they control our credit-based monetary system and own the Federal Reserve Bank.

Lately though, banks have captured the academic community and dominate Congress and our elected officials. Political lobbyists write our banking reform laws and buy politicians of both parties who willingly do their bidding.

Bank executives have their bonuses in mind, without regard for the risks they pose to the financial system. This is the background for the next financial crisis and a coming opportunity to buy real estate.

Real estate is tied to banking because it is credit dependent. Banks control credit. Watching developments in banking is essential to protecting your investment in real estate, especially if you rely on credit for your investment or development survival. If nothing else, the 10-year financial crisis cycle will involve banking and very likely the larger financial trading arena. Today it's all about trading profits and high risk in this fast-moving computer-dominated financial casino of Wall Street.

Where will financial instability strike next? It's

127

impossible to know for sure, but we can do a simple analysis and make an educated guess. There is a good reason for doing this little thought experiment. It involves three characteristics that may help you understand our unstable political economy.

1. Credit
2. Complexity
3. Ego

Credit refers to leveraged debt with little equity capital to absorb losses if prices drop or if the trend that supported the trade goes bad.

Complexity means that algorithms have replaced common sense and have given participants a misplaced trust in the mathematical models they use to make decisions.

Ego refers to the people taking the risk, who think they are the smartest because they have discovered how to eliminate the risks associated with high leverage.

Here we're looking for clues as to why our political economy is prone to instability and seeing if we can find an area that is likely to cause the next crisis. In the process, we're pointing to a way to keep financial crises to a minimum.

1. Credit: increase the capital requirements.
2. Complexity: simplify to the point of common sense.
3. Ego: prosecute offenders who break the law.

If we look back to the general instability that surfaces in 10-year cycles and isolate the financial area involved, maybe we can see whose turn is scheduled for the 2018 cycle.

In 1987, the stock market crashed, virtually overnight. One of the many causes thought to be at the root was programmed computer trading. There is always argument after the fact over the cause of a crisis, usually because of the complexity inherent in the event. Programmed trading designed to eliminate risk by automatic fast placement of trades was considered a significant cause of this crash.

In 1998, Long Term Capital Management failed at the attempt to trade options in a way that eliminated risk while maximizing leverage. This involved highly leveraged option derivatives spread across the globe to eliminate risk.

In 2008, the entire credit system collapsed. This crisis involved highly-leveraged securitization and the attempt to eliminate risk by using credit default swaps as a type of insurance policy that many of the participants didn't even begin to understand.

The attempt to eliminate risk appears to be a pattern that may actually contribute to causing financial crises. This process repeatedly develops into structures so complex that risk appears to be eliminated so that extreme leverage can be used to maximize profits without consequence. Yet, when the curtain is pulled back, we see that the wizards have done nothing but confuse themselves, damaged the economy, and must run to the government and taxpayers to be saved.

In 2018, where will the fast-moving leverage and unimaginable complexity created by unleashed egos hit the world of finance? Big banks are still likely candidates for a repeat performance because of their continuing efforts to hide what they do to make money—high leverage trading.

There is also another area that seems so out of control that it's difficult to imagine that it will even survive until the 2017-18 time frame—high-frequency trading. This new computerized botnet could turn on itself and shock the creators back to reality. We have had several mini-flash crashes of stocks already.

Maybe this computer-driven decision matrix is building for a grand finale by synchronizing with the banks to create some big fireworks. That's a duo to watch. No doubt there will be others developing soon. We can't tell exactly what will cause the next financial crisis or exactly what form it will take. But we can stay alert and informed.

What does this have to do with real estate? If a crisis involves credit and banks, it involves real estate. Our financial system is interlocked — anything that threatens the banking system and the flow of credit will touch real estate, including a stock market crash.

"No surprise" is the objective. If you can arrange your life so surprises are kept to a minimum, and the crises that come do not change your lifestyle, you can maintain stability in spite of our unstable political economy.

Holding onto Land

Ultimately, you must accumulate capital to be financially secure. But while you work toward that objective, arrange for a stable monthly income by keeping your day job and building income from rentals. Financial security requires both stable monthly income and capital investment. This is the advantage of rental investment, whether residential or commercial — it serves both purposes.

Also work to invest in land for long-term appreciation as you acquire income property. It's amazing how land bought 20 years from the edge of the city can provide financial security in one lump sum

---

when you might need it most. It's the way land is priced—by the square foot—that makes this possible.

For example, say you buy five acres for $3,000 an acre, which may seem high at the time. But the purchase can take on a completely different perspective in 20 years. Although you can't tell what the future holds, you can do an optimistic math calculation to help you define why it's good to hold onto land.

Five acres contains 217,800 square feet, which you purchase for $0.0689 per square foot. (5 x 43,560 = 217,800sf) ($3,000 / 43,560sf = $0.0689)

Let's say that about 20 years from the date of your purchase a major road is being built in front of your 5 acres and a developer wants to buy it for commercial use. She is willing to pay $4.75 per square foot. This works out to $1,034,550, ($4.75 x 217,800sf = $1,034,550). That's why it pays to hold onto land.

Following the Seventh Law

1. Owning real estate sustains hope.
2. Keep a balance between capital and cash flows.
3. You make your money when you buy.
4. Being active in the market is half the battle.
5. Learn to think critically.
6. Arrange your life for stability.
7. Stay alert.

If you would like more on the many ways to acquire real estate, you might find my other book helpful. It's available at Amazon.com: *Real Estate Acquisition: 150 Techniques for Serious Investors.*

Afterword

While the value of real estate is measured by the cash flow it generates, the security that comes from owning it is priceless. Investing in real estate has the advantage of leverage, which accelerates the accumulation of equity and, therefore, financial security and independence.

As you pursue the acquisition of real estate, keep the big picture of your life in mind. Then visualize it in the context of how the larger economy affects your financial security. We live in unstable times. Surprises can come at any time and from any direction. Work to structure your life so that no matter what happens, it will not change your chosen lifestyle.

Escape the trap of our consumer economy, lead a simple life, and avoid debt that does not produce income. Hold onto the money you have. Learn from your mistakes and improve. Conduct your life with compassion. Seek the right action at every decision point—it's not always obvious. Be kind. You never know what others are going through.

###